FLOWERS

MUSÉE DU LOUVRE

Henri Loyrette
President-Director

Didier Selles
Chief Executive Director

Catherine Sueur
Deputy Executive Director

Hervé Barbaret
Deputy Executive Director

Juliette Armand
Direction of Cultural Development

PUBLICATIONS

Musée du Louvre

Violaine Bouvet-Lanselle
Head of Publications
Series Editor

Camille Sourisse
Editorial Coordination

Fanny Meurisse
Photo Research

Flammarion

Sophy Thompson
Director, Illustrated Books

Translated from the French
by David Radzinowicz
Design: Isabelle Ducat
Copyediting: Penelope Isaac
Typesetting: Claude Olivier Four
Proofreading: Marc Feustel
Color Separation Reproscan, Italy
Printed in Malaysia by Tien Wah Press

AUTHORS

Michel Lis is editor-in-chief of the magazine *L'Ami des jardins* and contributes to *Rustica* in France where he is one of the most popular gardening presenters on French television and radio. He has published numerous gardening books.

Béatrice Vingtrinier is an art historian and worked for fifteen years at the Louvre, where she was in charge of the museum's educational workshops. She now gives lectures on the history of art at a number of Paris museums, including the Louvre, as well as the Musée d'Orsay, Musée Picasso, and Musée Rodin.

Editor's Note: All measurements of works are given in height by width unless otherwise indicated.

Distributed in North America by Rizzoli International Publications, Inc.

FLOWERS

IN THE LOUVRE

MICHEL LIS
BÉATRICE VINGTRINIER

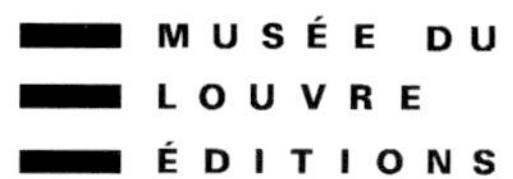

MUSÉE DU LOUVRE ÉDITIONS | Flammarion

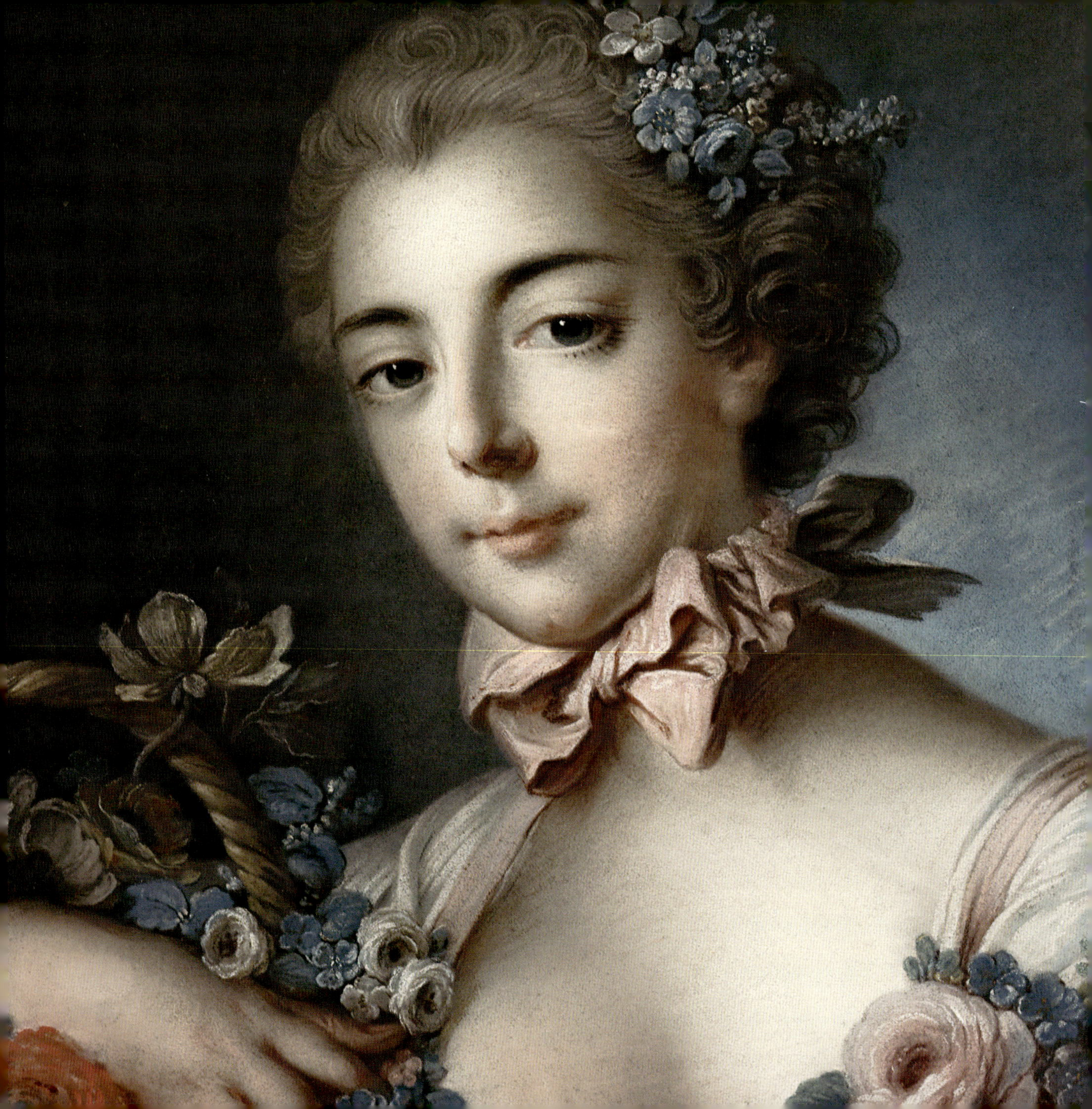

LET THE FLOWERS SPEAK!

by **Michel Lis**

FRANÇOIS BOUCHER
(1703–1770)
*Girl Holding a Basket
of Flowers*, 1756
Pastel on parchment,
17 ¼ x 14 ½ in.
(44 x 37 cm)

F lowers are like flightless butterflies that sway in the summer breeze. Firmly fixed in the nourishing earth by their roots, they do not run about in all directions as men do. This is why they strike such perfect poses before the painter's brush, sculptor's chisel, or engraver's burin. The present volume is full of delicious examples of this quality.

Whether wild or garden varieties, flowers, for the most part, seem touched by the wing of some god or demiurge. This is how the carnation was born: when Venus, jealous of the beauty of a young shepherd who dared spurn her, lost her temper. Tearing out his devastatingly beautiful if scornful eyes, she threw them on the wayside and there the first carnation bloomed.

Among the Greeks it was again our capricious Aphrodite who flew to the aid of the handsome Adonis; he'd been gorged by a wild boar in a forest and was lying awash in blood. She wanted to avoid staining her pretty feet and so put on a flower, an orchid now known as "Venus's slipper." And it was once again Aphrodite, when it was mooted she might have to marry Vulcan, the god of fire, who crammed a crown of violets over her head to cover the stench of her husband-to-be!

As for the rose, it either reveals the truth about life ("it's no bed of roses") or keeps the secrets of those present. *Sub rosa*'s the word! A rose-grower in Provins even suggested that "God made the rose when resting after the creation of woman."

The humble cornflower, enthroned in a pastoral bouquet, in fact bears an extraordinary message. It says: "I don't dare confess my love for you." This field annual and accomplice to the poppy can be bolder, though: worn by a woman at her bosom, the cornflower is intended to spark mad love. Victor Hugo, something of an expert on the matter, makes the point for us in *Les Orientales*: "Go, go, O young girls, and gather cornflowers among the wheat!"

Sometimes, worn at a Tahitian girl's ear or engraved on the sides of a vase, the reputation of these flowers—so readily portrayed by artists—precedes them. It is said, for instance, that a poppy freshly picked promptly withers on its stalk. This ephemeral flower, driven from the fields with doses of pesticide, is forced to make its home on railroad embankments and casts a melancholic black eye at the passing trains. In some parts of the countryside it is known as the "flower of the devil." When the demon adorns a woman's hair with such a flower, she is quickly liable to do the "devil's work." The field poppy was, however, once the hero of a mythical legend, that of Persephone, abducted from her mother Demeter—goddess of the Earth and Jupiter's sister—by Hades, lord of Hell, who wanted to marry her. Demeter's sorrow was such that soon every plant in the world withered and died. Zeus had to bring Persephone back from the underworld every spring in the shape of a poppy so that the fields and meadows might grow green again and flowers blossom anew.

Recreated with brush or chisel, flowers are favorite themes with artists. Singly or in sprays, they resemble gardens through which viewers can let their imagination wander unconstrained. One lone flower can, sometimes, by its grace and color, be more eloquent than a huge bunch.

The marquise de Pompadour drew and engraved fifty-three etchings; these were preceded by a frontispiece by François Boucher showing various blooms. Meanwhile the honest King Clovis chose the flower of the yellow iris of the marshes as an emblem for the royal currency, though it was quickly mixed up with the lily, the royal insignia. Venus, jealous of Juno who had just created that regal flower, hastened to stick an unprepossessing yellow nose in the middle of its snow-white corolla …

As a gardener, when I crisscross my domain, I zigzag over a carpet of flowers. If, on the off-chance, I halt in front of a heliotrope, I remember that this flower was customarily presented to a lady whose favors had already been obtained, and I promptly forget its botanical name (*Heliotropium*). It's a flower that should not be neglected and which enchanted Marcel Proust in *Jean Santeuil*: "You know of course that it is when it is drenched by the rain that one can truly take in the fresh scent of lilac, while the heliotrope offers the fullness of its sweet fragrance only to the sun."

Flowers possess scents and colors that are more delicate than their Greek or Latin names, as the nineteenth-century writer, Alphonse Karr, put it in a startling definition: "The art of botany is to dry flowers between the pages of a dictionary and insult them in Greek and Latin."

It is said that it was Muhammad himself who "invented," or created, the jasmine, the true symbol of Islam, as well as the geranium. The gods of Olympus had made Hebe (the *veronica*) their wine-waiter to serve the fruit of Bacchus's vines at the banquets of Zeus. The god of gods himself was not above bestrewing his bed with saffron flowers to arouse the passions of the nymphs he wanted to seduced.

But there are still more flowery legends to impart … The beautiful gillyflower was born from the devotion of a young Scottish girl to her lover. After her father locked her up in a tower, she threw herself out of a window and perished at the feet of her beloved. At this very spot the first wallflower sprang up, which since then has symbolized faithfulness until death in the language of flowers.

The delicate flowers of the fields, which are so hard to grow in prison-like gardens, were the first to appear on earth. Well before mankind arrived, they were already waving in Zephyr's gentle breath or in Boreas's northerly blast, which strips and freezes the imprudent early flowering anemone. They dance on the wayside and in the meadows. "They are the puppets of God," a poet might add before opening his box of watercolors to capture their subtle hues. Valued or neglected, flowers only die, like the verbena in Sully-Prudhomme's poem, in vases broken by a blow from a fan. And who knows, perhaps some painter had already depicted a bouquet on the murderous fan?

The collection of vellums in the Natural History Museum in Paris presents an unequalled palette of colorful blooms in a collection from which the Botanical Gardens developed. During the reign of Henry IV of France, at this very spot, there stretched—between the River Bièvre where the tanners worked and the Seine—a vast garden cultivated by a skilful horticulturist whose neighbor made soft furnishings and was always on the lookout for new tints for his products that would be processed by the dyers on Rue de Bièvre. One day, the furnisher asked his friend to create some new colors for him, so the gardener had even more plants collected from the world over. A few years later and the Royal Garden was born. The painters of the time were among the first to show an interest in the previously unseen hues of these new flowers.

A popular tradition in Burgundy—sometimes practiced with mischievous intent—consisted in going at night to a beauty's window without her knowledge and tying a bloom, bouquet, or flowering branch to it. Thus the next day everyone was apprised of whether the recipient of the flowery offering enjoyed a good or bad reputation: whether she was faithful or flighty, a chatterbox, of worthy or worthless character, or even a "rose-bush" that had "lost its bloom" in "celebrating Easter before Palm Sunday," as they still say in the countryside.

In painting there exists an unspoken rule: only living and freshly picked blooms are depicted. A petal lain on the heart of the flower serves to show it is dead. Painters and gardeners, poets and moralists want only one thing: to let the flowers speak for themselves.

As they admire these works, viewers will doubtless have eyes only for the flowers the artist has painted and will cast scarcely more than a cursory glance at the person holding them or the beautiful woman they adorn. Flowers are the focus of our attention in a garden, and, as one of our greatest landscape designers, the Breton Erwan Tymen—whose designs specialize almost exclusively in foliage of all kinds—has observed: "A flower in a garden is like a whore on the sidewalk—people look only at her!" The language may be florid, but it reflects a reality I've seen for myself a hundred times. Flowers are essential in art, of course, as in daily life. What artist can resist the sight of a woman returning from market with a bouquet—sometimes thrown together rather hurriedly—sticking out of a basket overflowing with fruit and vegetables?

The collection that follows also shows how flowers have played a role in history: in his youth, Lazare Carnot, the great Carnot, was a member of a secret society, the Rosati of Arras, founded in 1778: his descendant, Sadi Carnot, was to become president of the Republic.

Let us salute the Persian poet Saadi, who wrote the longest poem on roses (twenty thousand lines); and Magloire, Robespierre's secretary, who, in fleeing the Terror after the death of the Incorruptible, took refuge with a Parisian horticulturist, where he was infected with such a passion for roses that he bred a variety himself.

A few years later and the five members of the Directory held sway in France, and roses had become a great favorite with the dandified (male) "*Inc[r]oyables*" and (female) "*Me[r]veilleuses*" (they didn't like to pronounce the "r" of "Revolution"!). Then, in France, came the imperial violets of Napoleon I, the carnations of the Restoration and the Royalists (and the "Carnation" Revolution that brought democracy back to Portugal), the field poppy, symbol of the French Army in the First World War, and, lest one forget, the Wars of the Roses, in which the houses of Lancaster and York fought for the English throne (1455–1487). Closer to the present-day, there's the rose clenched in a fist.

In spite of such partisanship, flowers remain doggedly independent and can still translate the sweet supplications of the troubadours into the language of love. (Philippe) Fabre d'Eglantine added the "wild rose" (eglantine) to his patronym off his own bat before coming up with the horticulturally themed months of the Republican calendar: Floréal, Germinal, Prairial, Messidor.

Painters understand all this very well, and continue to decorate their subjects with the eternal symbol of the flower. The enigma of their fragrance remains intact. As the dramatist Henry de Montherlant observed: "Scent is the intelligence of flowers."

SELECTED WORKS

Text by
Béatrice Vingtrinier

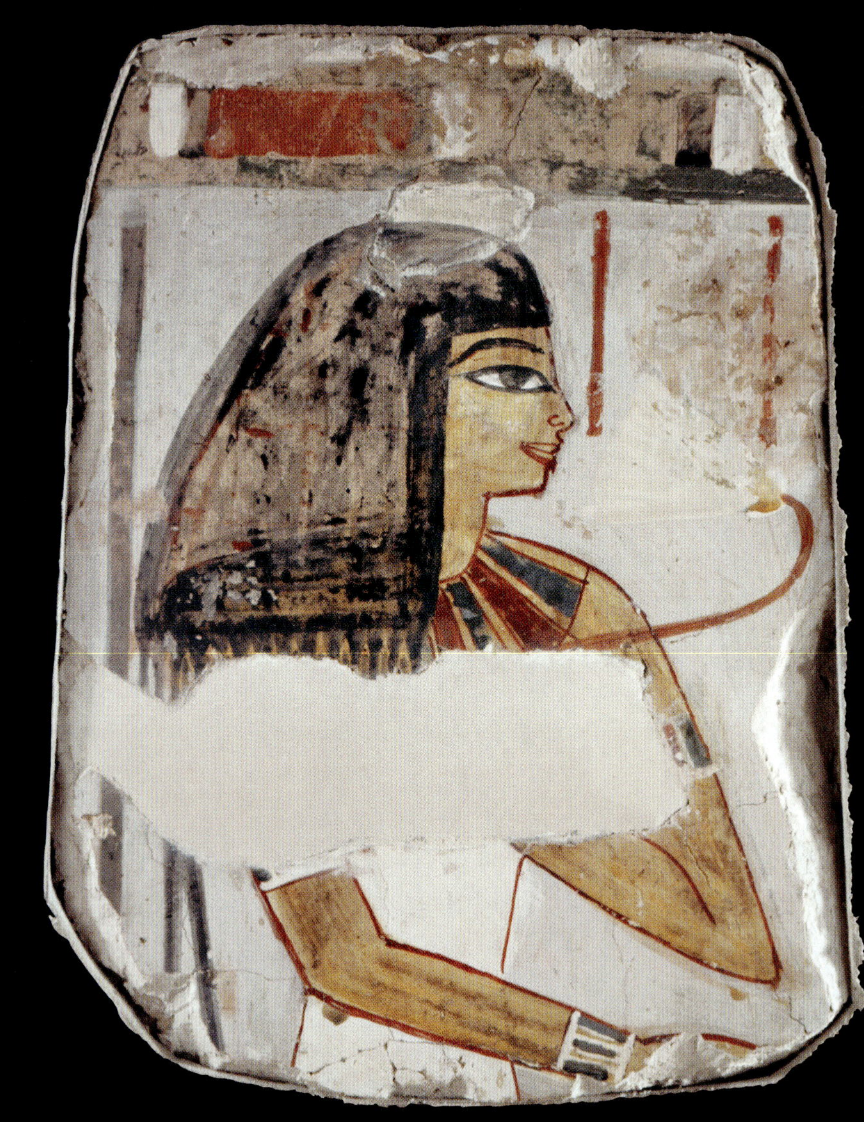

1. *Wall painting, Woman smelling a lotus flower*
1550–1295 BCE, Eighteenth Dynasty
Loess, straw, 13 ¾ x 10 ½ x 1 in.
(35 x 26.7 x 2.6 cm)

2. *Stele of Lady Taperet*
Tenth or ninth century BCE, Twelfth Dynasty or
Third Intermediate Period
Paint and varnish on wood, 12 ¼ x 11 ½ x 1 in.
(31 x 29 x 2.6 cm)

1. Two varieties of lotus exist in Egypt:
the fragrant blue lotus (*Nymphaea caerulea*)
and the white lotus (*Nymphaea lotus*).
Botanists today prefer to keep this
designation for the *Nelumbo*, which comes
from India and which was unknown
in Egypt before the Persian era. (The term
employed by French Egyptologists is
"nénufar" with an "f" because the word
has Egyptian roots and not Greek, as the
spelling "nénuphar" might imply.)

One of the Egyptian versions of
the creation of the world, the cosmogony
of Hermopolis, recounts how the sun was
born from a lotus in the shape of a child.
This association of the sun and the lotus
flower derives from the observation that
the petals of these plants, which grow so
abundantly on the banks of the Nile, remain
closed in the evening and open
only in the morning. The lotus is a symbol of
the rebirth of life and its many
representations in a funerary context
(as here) feature a figure breathing in
its scent, as it is supposed to restore life.
Thanks to the magical emanations of this
flower dedicated to the sun, this elegant
woman from the New Empire will surely
keep her youth and beauty for all eternity.

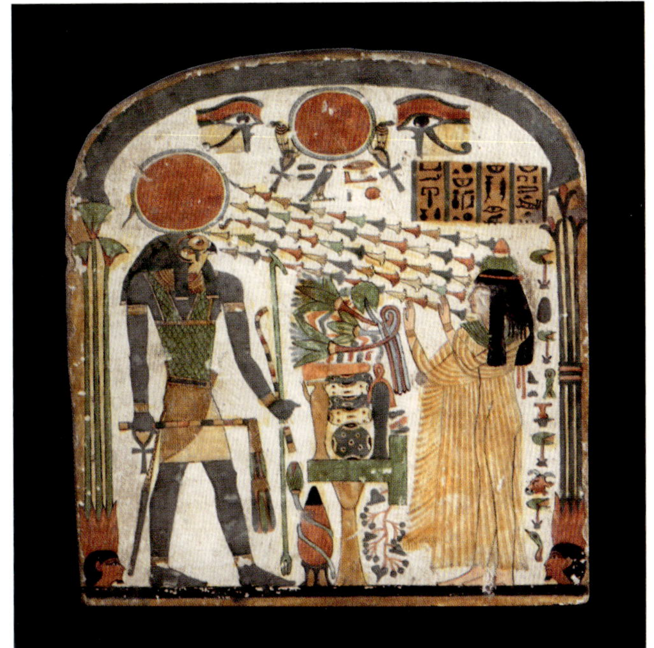

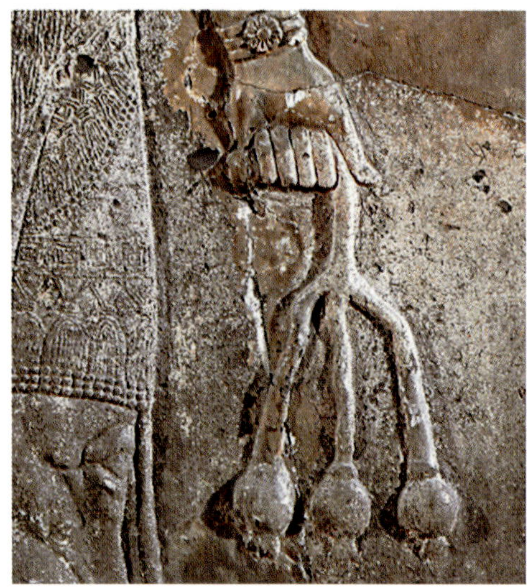

This relief of the neo-Assyrian era was discovered in a building near the palace of Sargon II in Khorsabad—the Dur-Sharrukin of Antiquity and the second capital of the Assyrian Empire, erected in the eighteenth century BCE. It features a theme frequent in Assyrian art: the sacred tree, a symbol of the balance of the universe, flanked by two genii offering blessings. The second genius that should have appeared on the right is missing. The surviving figure grasps a stem, from which sprout three stylized poppy capsules, while the other hand is raised in a sign of invocation.

Originating in Asia before being introduced into the Mediterranean Basin, the opium poppy (*Papaver somniferum*) has been known for thousands of years. The Sumerians were acquainted with it and it is probably this that is described as the "plant of joy" on a cuneiform tablet from Nippur, which presents a list of medical remedies in the form of a prescription and dates from the end of the third millennium. In addition to its importance in medicine, the poppy seems to have been employed in a religious context. The Ancients were clearly aware of its soporific effects and knew how to extract opium from the capsules: hence this species of poppy became the symbol of drowsiness and forgetfulness, and the attribute of all divinities concerned with sleeping and dreaming, such as Morpheus. Finally, it was associated with the eternal sleep and hence with death.

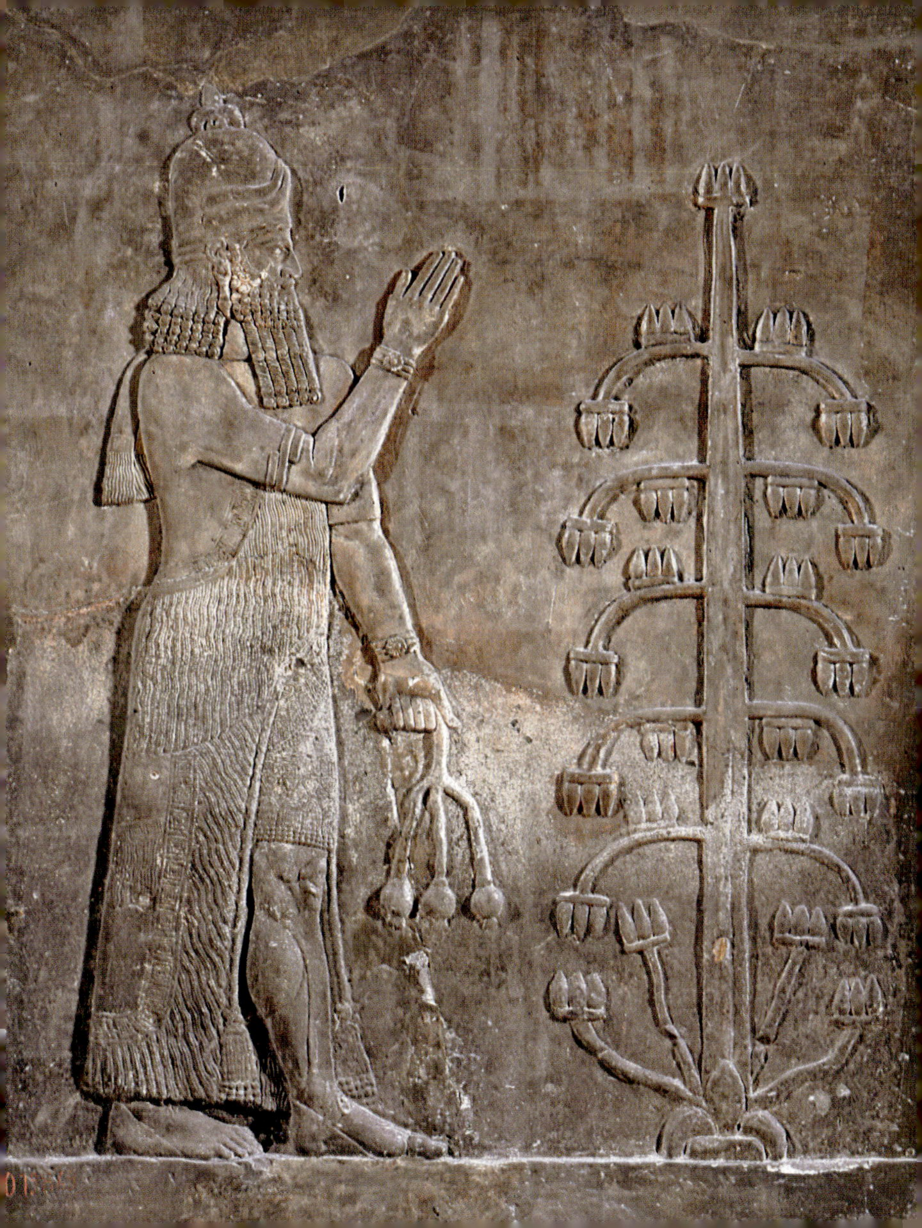

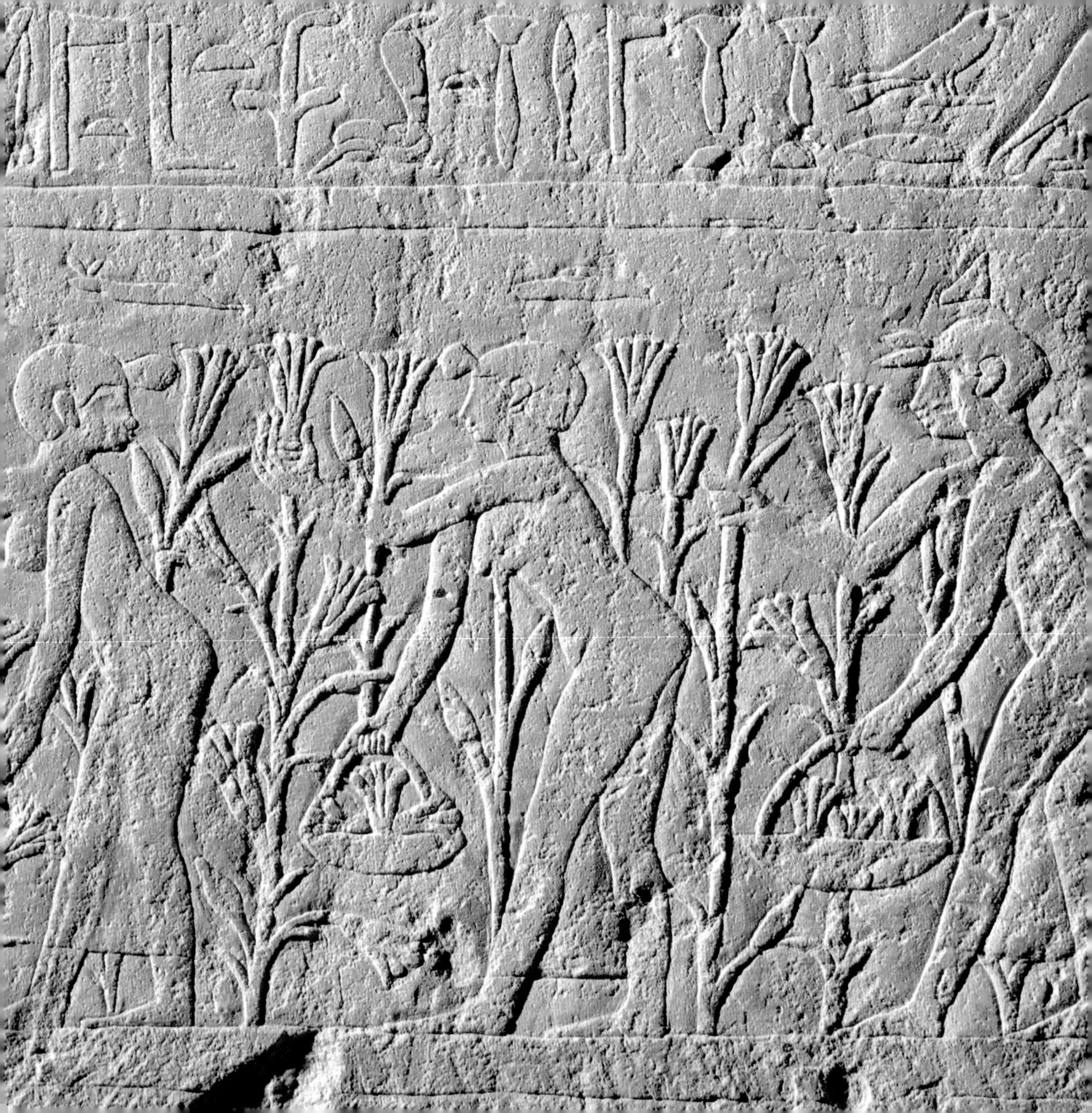

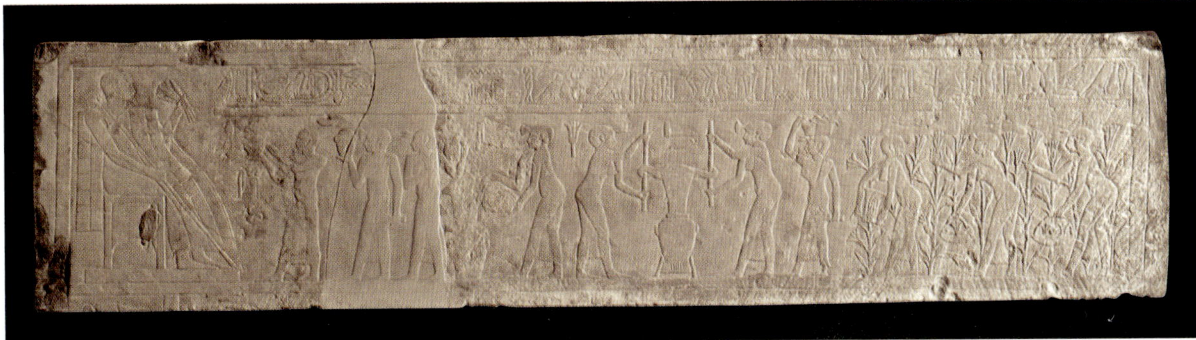

"Lirinon" Relief from the tomb of Pairkep; Preparing perfume from lilies
Reign of Psammetic II? (595–589 BCE), Twenty-sixth Dynasty
Limestone, 11 ½ x 46 ¾ x 3 ¼ in. (29 x 119 x 8 cm)

Flowers fulfill an essential role in composing perfumes. Carved with a delicate bas-relief, this lintel from the tomb of Pairkep (Egypt, Twenty-sixth Dynasty) shows various stages in the preparation of a fragrance from the lily. On the right, three women pick the flowers while a fourth brings in the blooms in a Moses basket balanced on her head. The liquid is then extracted by wringing the flowers in a piece of cloth twisted between two sticks; the juice obtained flows into the large earthenware jar underneath. One essential stage in the extraction of the fragrance is omitted from the relief, however: the maceration of the plants in oil prior to drying. On the left, a man named in the hieroglyphic text as an "inspector" hands a cup to the owner of the tomb.

The relief provides little information on how this product, known as "lirinon," was used and whether it was medicinal or aromatic. It is known that the Egyptians were hugely fond of scented substances of all kinds and from the earliest dynasties archaeology and contemporary texts alike attest to the use of perfumed balsams, ointments, and oils to firm up the skin or keep the hair silky. Some cosmetics were in addition believed to have prophylactic or medical properties. In the end, the exact contents of the cup here hardly matters since, by the magical power the Egyptians lent to such depictions in tombs, Pairkep will have this luxury product at his disposal for all eternity!

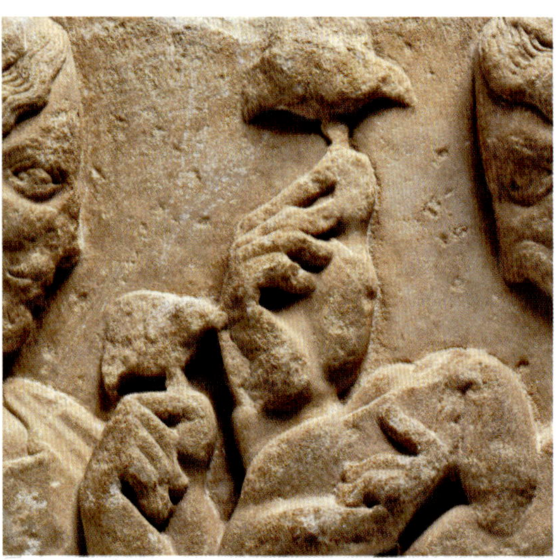

With their faces in strict profile, two women gaze into each other's eyes in eternal contemplation. Did the figures originally sit or stand? No one can be sure: the stele is broken and the lower parts of the women's bodies have long since vanished. In the center of the composition, three hands emerge from the flaps of their thick mantles, fastened at the shoulder; the hands form an elegant bouquet. Each figure holds a garden poppy or pomegranate flower in the right hand and a small sachet perhaps containing seeds in the left. It was because Persephone stole a few pomegranate seeds from Hades that she is imprisoned in the underworld for part of the year. This cruelty plunges her mother Demeter into such a fit of sorrow that the goddess keeps all land infertile for the months she is unable to see her daughter. The *papaver* poppy too was an attribute of Demeter as she would assuage the sadness caused by the loss of Persephone with opium. The identity of the two women here nevertheless remains a mystery: is the relief a votive one representing Kore and Demeter, goddesses both connected to the cycle and rebirth of the vegetal world? More likely the fragment comes from a funerary stele that shows in the same scene the deceased in the company of one of her relations, with the flowers and seeds perhaps evoking a future resurrection, a mortuary context that would explain the hint of melancholy in their expression.

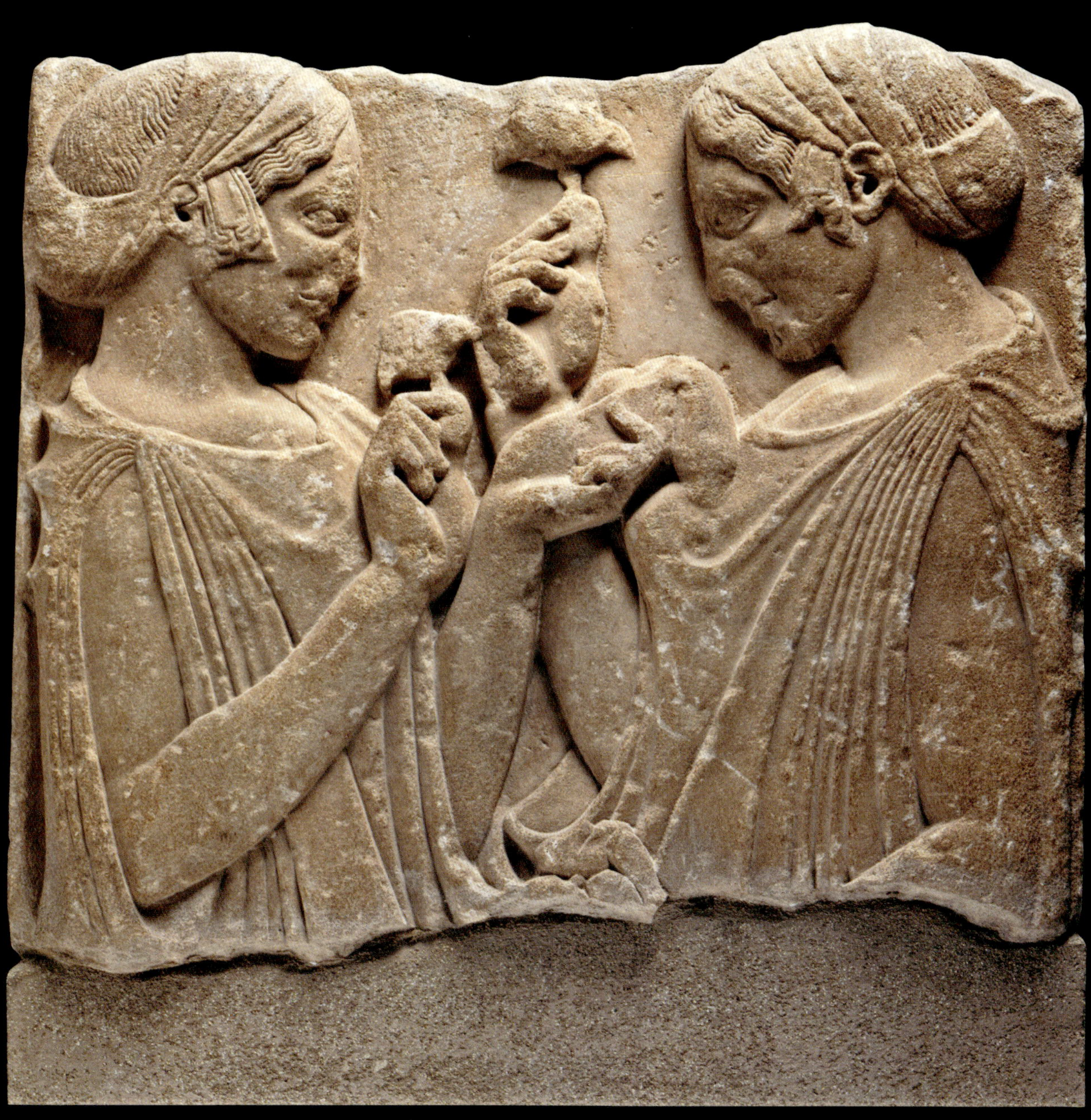

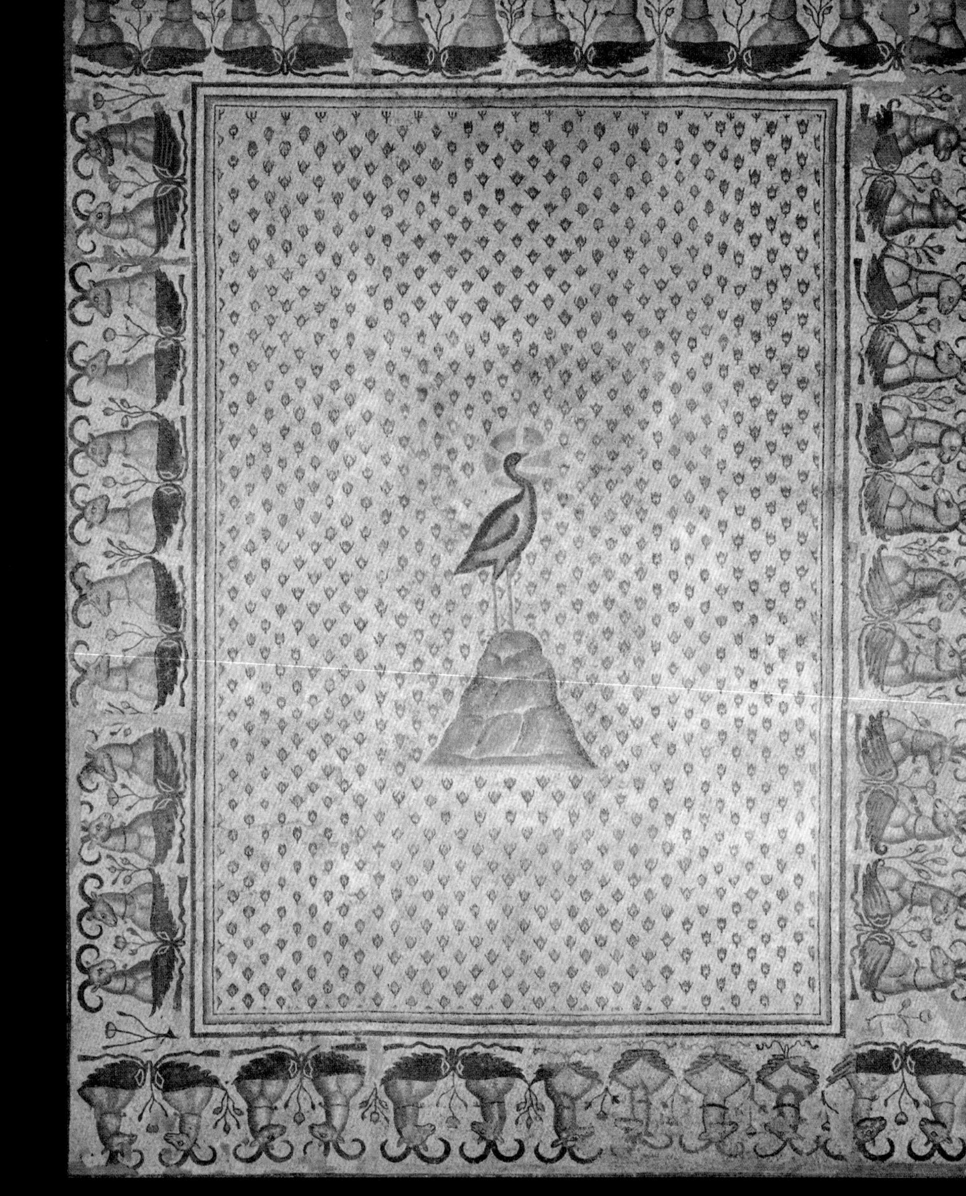

Fragment of a floor mosaic: scattering of roses and Phoenix
Late fifth century CE.
Marble and limestone, 19 ft. 8 ¼ in. x 13 ft. 11 ¼ in. (6 x 4.25 m)

This pavement mosaic once adorned an open-air courtyard in a large house of the Hellenistic period at Daphne in Syria. In the center, a pattern of rose blooms is scattered about a phoenix whose head is ringed by a halo. Originally from a far larger composition, the best-preserved fragments from this floor mosaic were relaid at a later date. Before it was reassembled, this repetitive décor that must have brought a measure of unity to the courtyard numbered no less than 7,500 roses!

Without question the "queen of flowers," the rose has been appreciated for its beauty and celebrated by poets and writers since Antiquity. Mythology teaches us that the flower was created by the goddess Flora out of the lifeless body of a nymph. Herodotus (484–425 BCE) explains how the rose was imported into Greece from Asia Minor by King Midas, who left his land of Phrygia for exile in Macedonia with a sixty-petal rose in his luggage. In the first century CE, Pliny the Elder was already describing twenty varieties of rose bush in his *Natural History*. In Rome, no festival or banquet was complete without roses: Romans put its petals into their wine and scented their baths with them, and they would be thrown over illustrious guests like confetti. It was even said that Cleopatra and Mark Antony first made love on a bed strewn with rose petals to a depth of a foot and a half!

The flower's destiny, though, was a curious one: once a stalwart of every Roman orgy, by the Middle Ages it had been transformed into a symbol of purity and, combined with columbine and carnation, now referred to the inviolable chastity of the Virgin Mary.

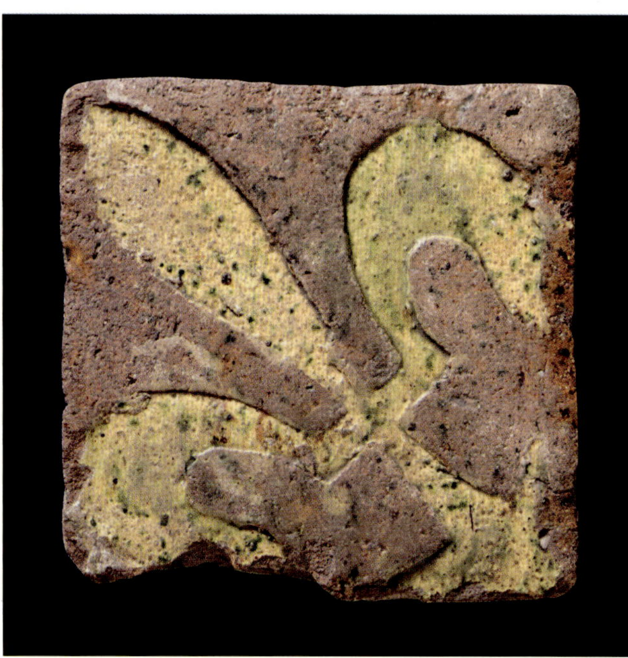

1. *Paving stone: Fleur-de-lis*
Thirteenth–fourteenth century
Glazed earthenware, h. 5 in. (12.5 cm)

2. *Clasp decorated with a fleur-de-lis,*
known as the *"Fermail de Saint Louis"*
Mid-fourteenth century
Silver-gilt, champlevé enamel, semi-
precious stones, h. 7 in. (18 cm) approx.

1. Historians are still not agreed as to
the significance of the choice of the lily
(the fleur-de-lis) as an heraldic symbol
of the kings of France. Though
such discussions can be left to specialists,
it should be recalled that the blazon *Azur
semé de fleurs de lys d'or* was adopted
definitively during the reign of Philippe-
Auguste. Perhaps in this way the king
of France shared his emblem with the
Virgin, thereby accentuating the religious
dimension of the monarchical function
acquired at the consecration.

2. This diamond-shape *fermail* (clasp) comes
from the royal treasury of Saint-Denis and
is adorned with a lily flower in precious
stones mounted on silver gilt. The black
enamel ground is also strewn with
fleurs-de-lis. Such a scattering (*semé* in
heraldic terms) is redolent of a starry sky,
a cosmic image that seeks to underline the
special link the French monarchy maintains
with God. With the advent of the Valois,
these "lys *semés*" will gradually be replaced
by three large lily blooms arranged in
a form that endured until the collapse of
the Ancien Régime. In consequence, French
kings could boast not only the protection
of the Virgin but also of the Trinity.

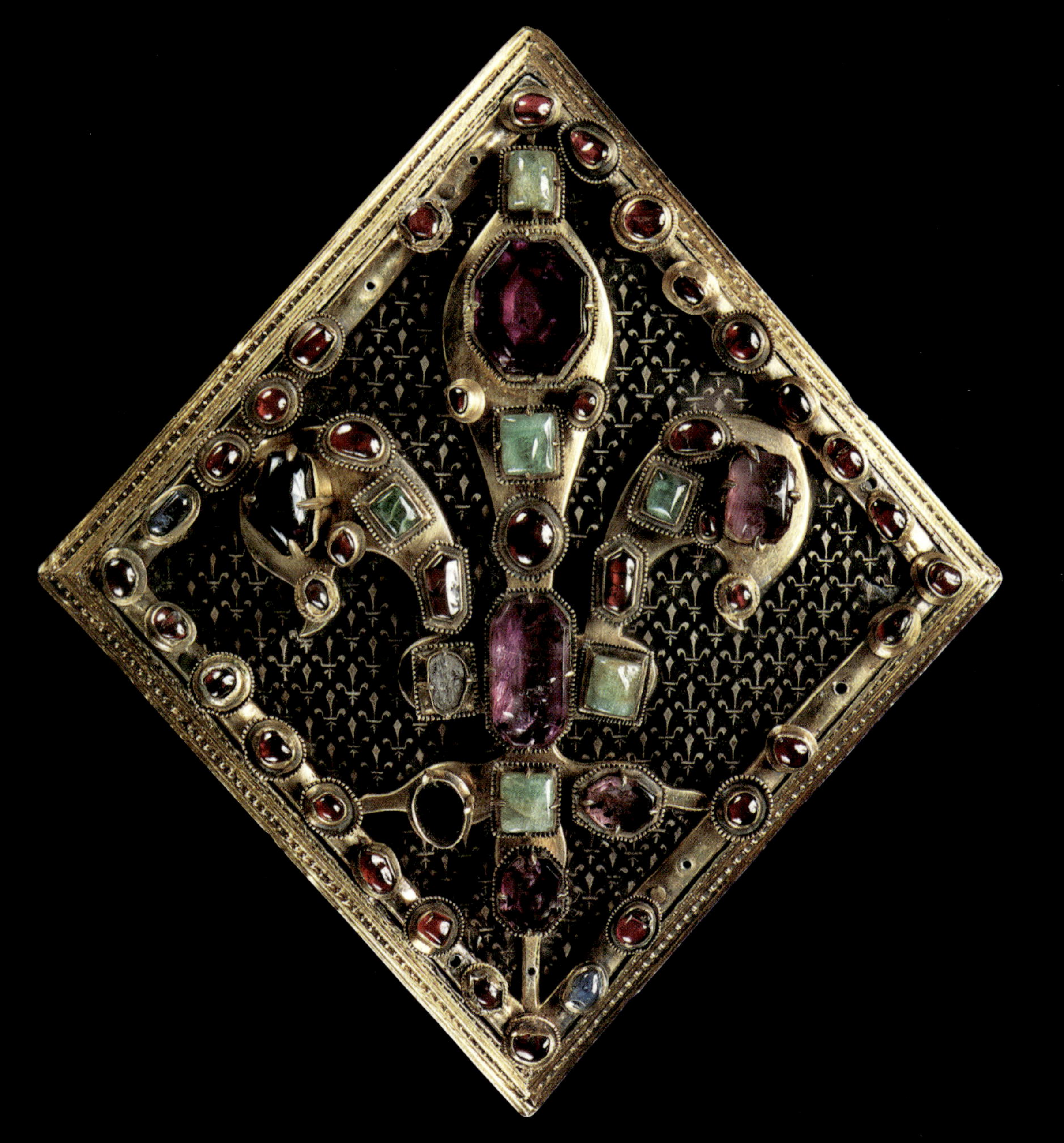

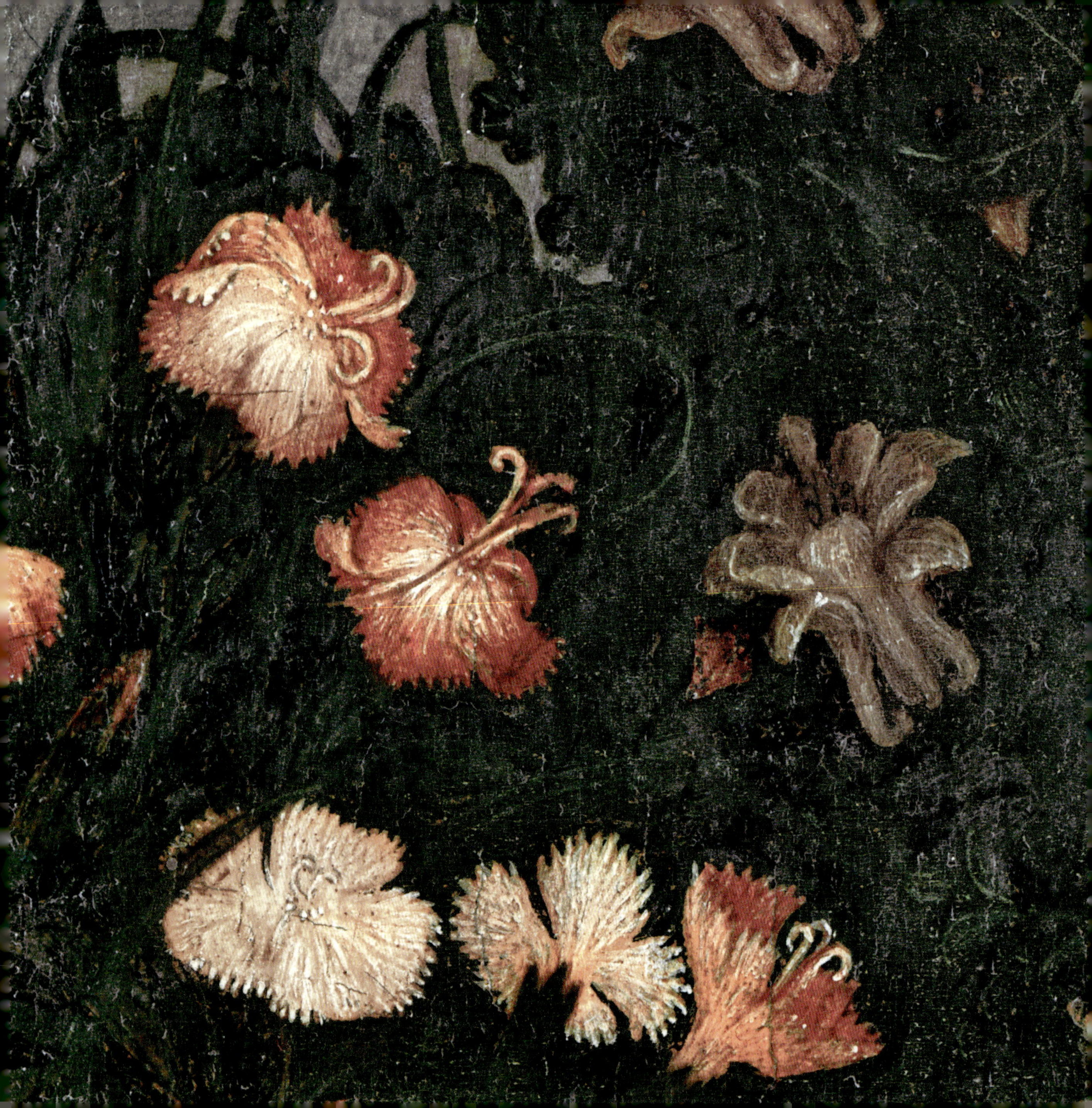

ANTONIO PUCCIO, *CALLED* PISANELLO
(c. 1395–1455)
Portrait of a Young Princess, c. 1435–1440
Oil on wood, 17 x 11 ¾ in. (43 x 30 cm)

Who could this young princess be?
The elaborate crystal vase studded
with small pearls embroidered on her sleeve
is an emblem of the d'Este family, whose
house reigned in Ferrara. She is attired
in a white dress arranged so as to leave
the red puff sleeves and green belt exposed.
Recurring in the trim on her garment,
these three colors belong to the Gonzaga
family of Mantua. Certain historians see the
branch of juniper in piqué at the sleeve-hole
as proof that this must be a portrait of
Ginevra d'Este, since in fifteenth-century
Italian the plant was known as *ginevero*; this
little sprig would thus be an *arme parlante,*
representing her name by way of a visual
"pun." Yet, as the juniper tree was also
considered a symbol of peace and happiness,
its presence might possess a broader meaning
than simply the forename of Ginevra.
Likewise, the colors of the d'Este family
emblem and those of the Gonzagas might
just as easily point to Lucia d'Este, who
married Carlo Gonzaga, or else Margherita
Gonzaga, wife of Leonello d'Este.

The exact identity of the model, though,
surely matters less than the charm of the
portrait. Pisanello, who earned his spurs
as a medalist, captures the girl's features
and profile in neat, flowing lines. These
decorative arabesques—where elegance is
more important than the psychology of the
sitter—emerge from a ground of which a
medieval tapestry-weaver might be justly

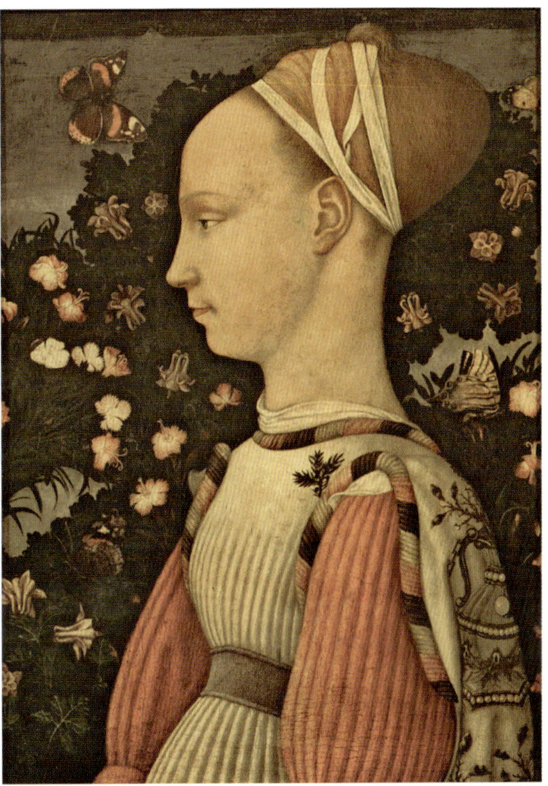

proud, so much do the butterflies and
flowers (pinks and columbines) dotted about
the dark green field remind one of the great
arrases of the period. If one is to believe
the language of flowers, this picture might
well celebrate an engagement or a wedding:
the carnation symbolizes a marriage promise
or marital fidelity and, if the columbine
often refers to the Passion of Christ, it speaks
of a quite different passion when associated
with a female portrait.

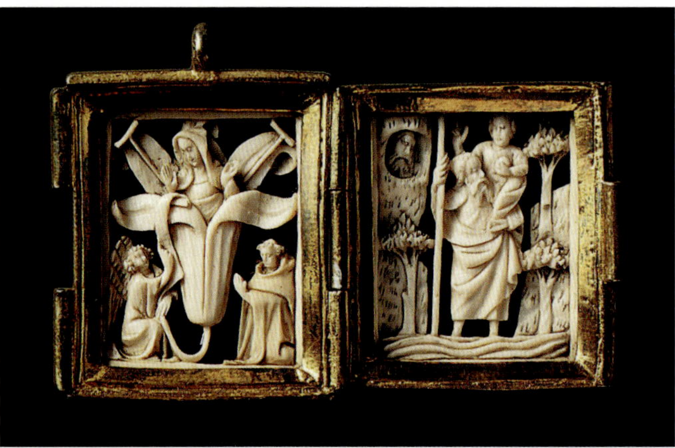

1. *Diptych: Annunciation, St Christopher*
Second half of the fifteenth century
Silver-gilt, ivory, 1 x 1 ¾ in. (2.8 x 4.5 cm)

2. **ROGIER VAN DER WEYDEN** (c. 1399/1400–1464)
The Annunciation, c. 1440
Oil on wood, 33 ¾ x 36 ½ in. (86 x 93 cm)

1. Carved in ivory, this small diptych, which could be worn as a piece of jewelry, presents an Annunciation with a somewhat unusual iconography. Nearly the entire field of the composition is occupied by a huge lily, from which emerges, between two pistils and four petals, a Virgin in a state half of rapture and half of astonishment.
To either side of this striking scene, the Archangel Gabriel and a tonsured monk seem almost crushed—or perhaps just sheltered—by the flower's gigantic corolla.

2. Originating in the Orient, the white lily (*Lilium candidum L.*) was long cultivated both for its ornamental beauty and sweetish scent. In medieval gardens, it was often grown in conjunction with the rose. Very early on it acquired religious connotations which, in the early Middle Ages, were mainly Christological in nature, before becoming more closely associated with the Virgin at the turn of the millennium as the Marian cult spread. The lily then became a symbol of purity and virginity. Indeed, if the dogma of the Immaculate Conception was only officially enshrined in the nineteenth century, Mary was already regarded as exempt from Original Sin in the feudal era. The lily is the prerequisite flower in any work representing the Annunciation. In the painting by Rogier van der Weyden, three lilies in a vase symbolize the triple virginity of Mary, before, during, and after the birth of Christ.

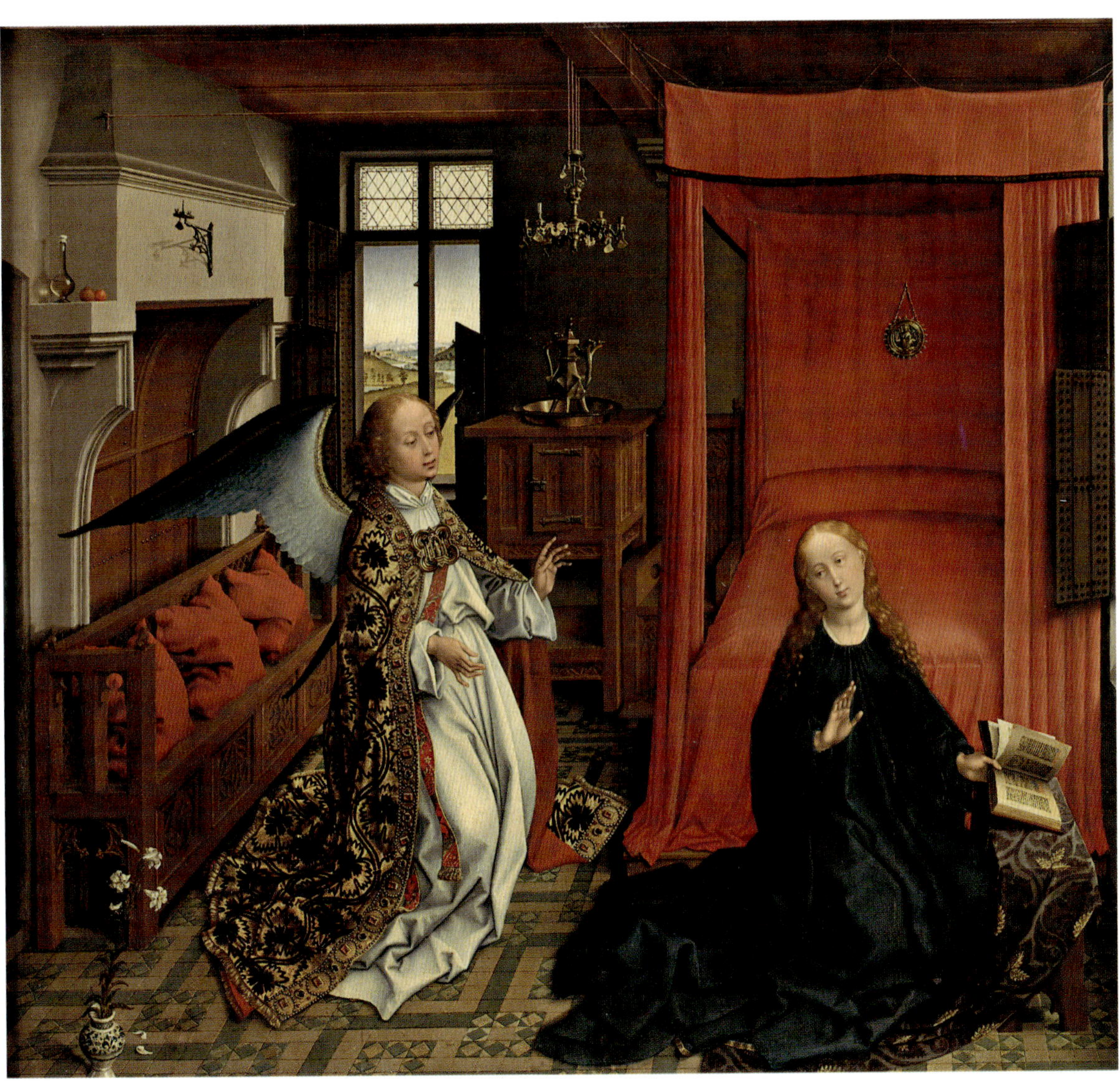

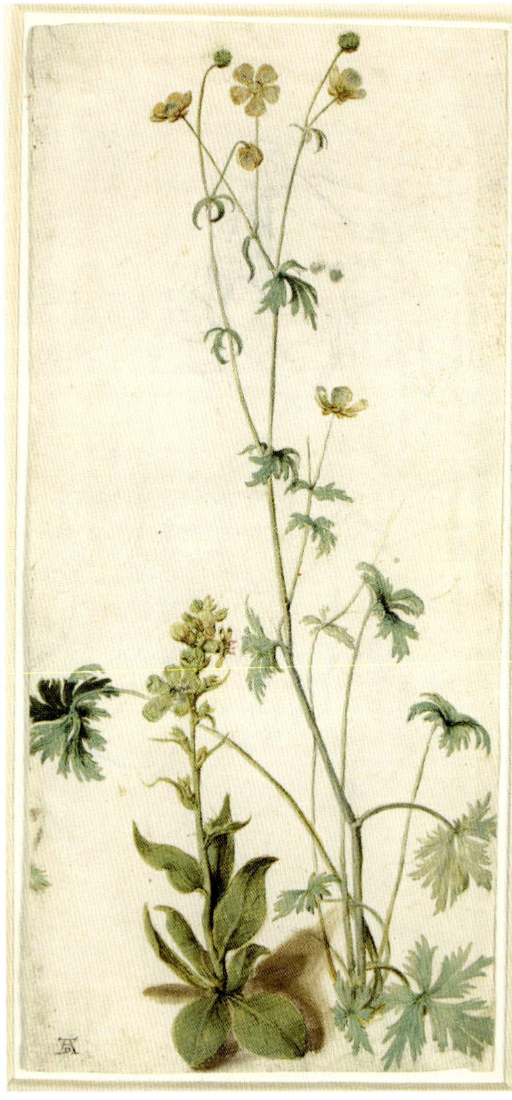

1. **ALBRECHT DÜRER** (1471–1528)
A Flower, n.d.
Watercolor, pen, and brown ink,
11 ¾ x 5 ½ in. (30 x 13.7 cm)

2. **ALBRECHT DÜRER** (1471–1528)
Portrait of the Artist Holding a Thistle, 1493
Oil on wood, 22 x 17 ¼ in. (56 x 44 cm)

2. The year is 1493: Dürer is twenty-two and has just unveiled his first painted self-portrait, thereby testifying to a taste for self-questioning that was to last his entire life. Eschewing all preparatory drawing, he reproduces his features straight on the parchment as he observed them in a mirror. The three-quarter view against a dark ground follows the traditional template of this type of self-portrait.

Two verses are inscribed in the upper section next to the date: *"My sach die gat/ Als es oben schtat"* ("My actions will conform to what is ordained on high"). In the foreground in his right hand, which was completed at a later stage, the painter holds out a sea-holly flower, a kind of thistle whose German name is *"Männertrau"* ("manly faithfulness"), a probable allusion to his forthcoming marriage to Agnes Frey. Moreover, in traditional Christian iconography, the plant is another symbol of the Passion and the Redemption, echoing the inscription that conveys the artist's determination to place his destiny in the hands of God.

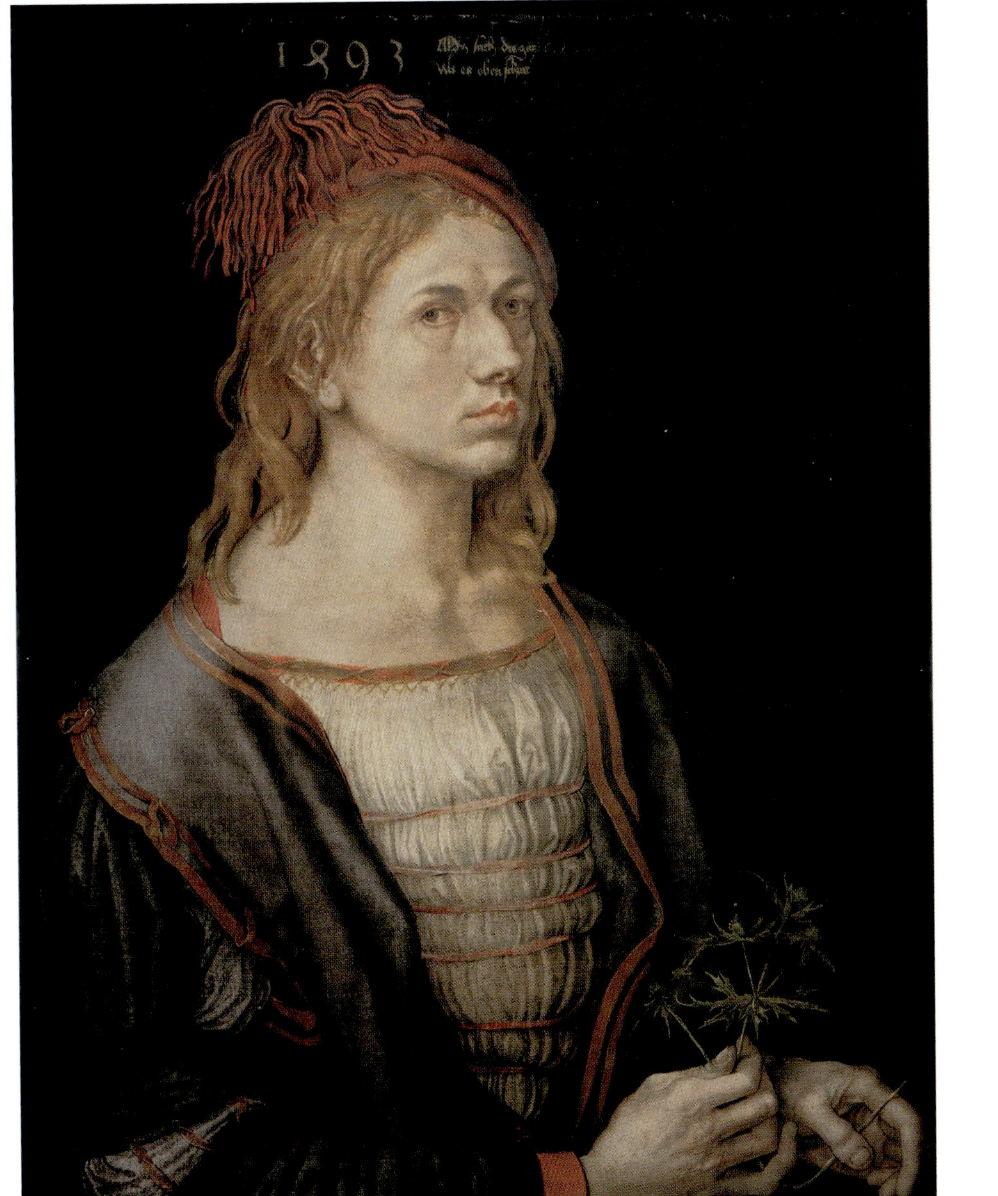

1493
My sach die gat
Als es oben schtat

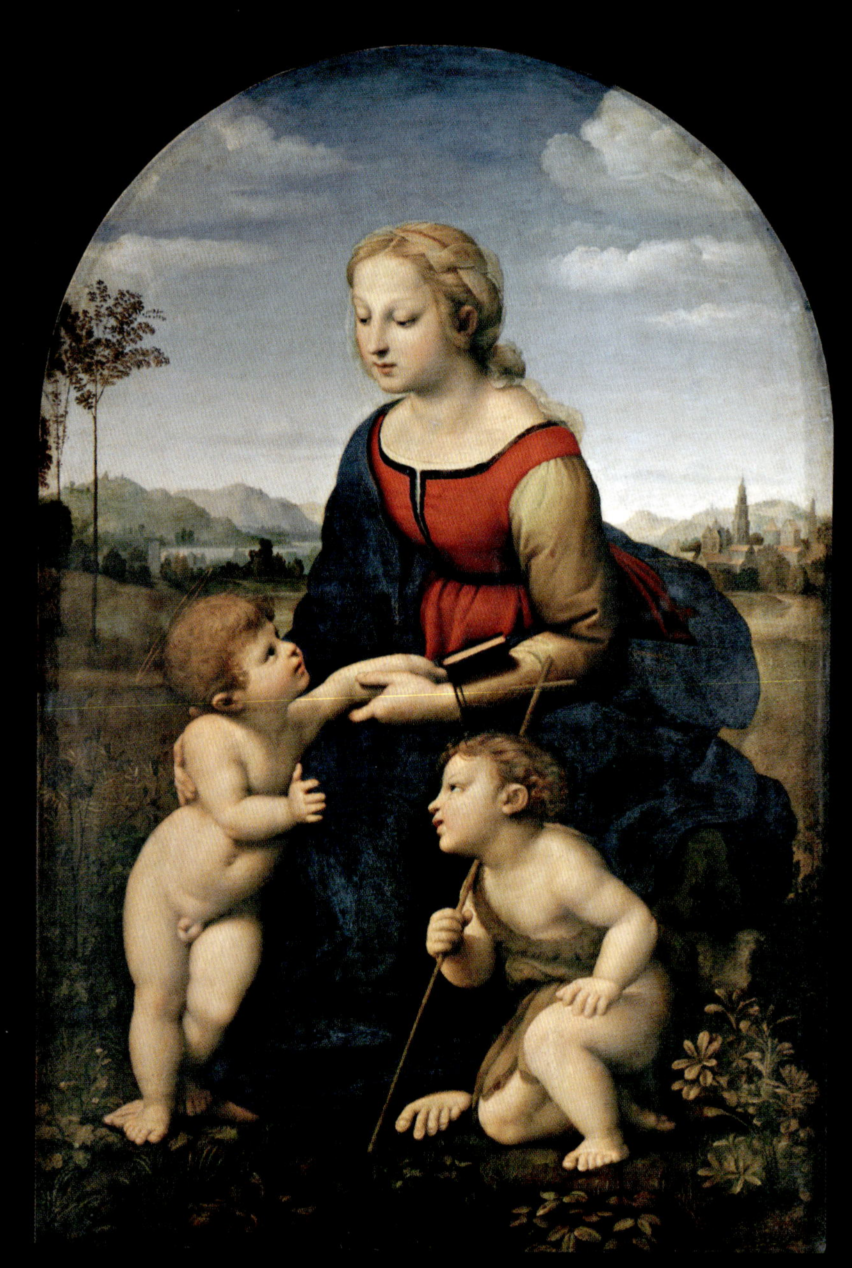

1. RAFFAELLO SANTI, *CALLED* RAPHAEL
(1483–1520)
Madonna and Child with St. John the Baptist, known as *La Belle Jardinière*,
c. 1507–1508
Oil on wood, 48 x 31 ½ in. (122 x 80 cm)

2. BERNARDINO LUINI (c. 1480/1490–1532)
Madonna and Child with an Angel, known as the *Madonna of Menaggio*, c. 1520–1530
Oil on wood, 31 ½ x 22 ¾ in. (80 x 58 cm)

1. & 2. In a serene Umbrian landscape bathed in a blond-tinged, even light, time seems to stand still in one final moment of innocent happiness before Jesus seizes the book in which his future Passion is announced. In the foreground, in a meadow surrounding the figures, the plants minutely delineated by the painter each carry a symbolic message.

Among the flowers carpeted over the ground, the discreet and almost invisible violet is associated with modesty, even timidity. Here it points to the humility of the Virgin Mary and of Jesus Christ, who was made Man. The columbine, meanwhile, due to the assonance of the French name, *ancolie*, with the word "melancholy," translates the sufferings of the Virgin and also forms part of the iconography of Christ's Passion. As for the trifoliate leaf of the strawberry plant, that can allude to the Trinity, while its white flowers are an image of innocence and its red-colored fruit evokes blood and also symbolizes the Passion.

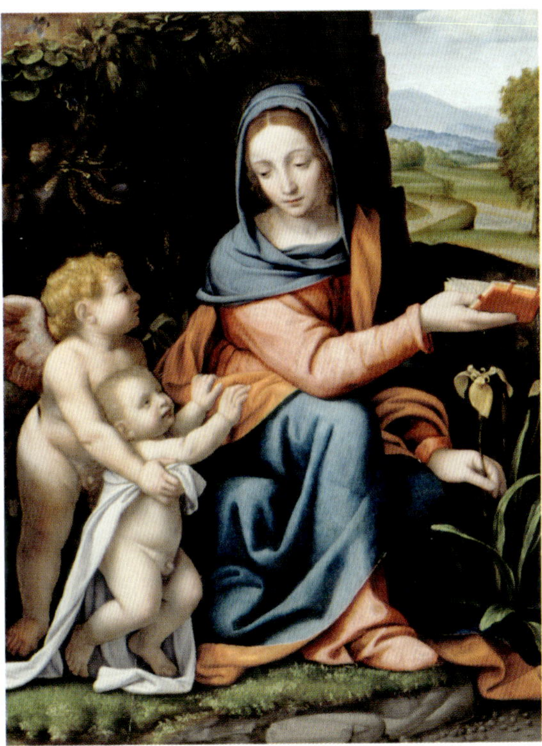

Characterized by a regular arrangement of leaves and a scattering of flowers over a plain ground, the kind of tapestry called mille-fleur came into its own in the fifteenth century and at the beginning the sixteenth. These arrases do not purport to afford a realistic representation of a medieval garden, but the absence of perspective reflects their principal characteristic in the Middle Ages: all such gardens were walled, closed in on themselves and spurning all views to the outside. Spaces where nature was domesticated, in which plants, animals, and men could live in harmony, they symbolize paradise, that perfect garden, scrupulously maintained and free of the brambles of sin. There, flowers would sing the praises of the bounty of the Lord who created all these splendid species, beautiful to look at or good to eat. Places of meditation in monasteries or of leisure in princely houses, such gardens were generally composite and comprised a square planted with herbs—including tinctorial, aromatic, culinary, and medicinal species; a kitchen garden; an orchard (that acted more a pleasure garden), and a flowery meadow. It was this last category—a meadow strewn with wild flowers—that inspired tapestries of the mille-fleur variety. They played host to the same wild species that flourished in hedgerows and fields: foxgloves, cowslips, snowdrops, daisies, periwinkles, violets, lilies of the valley, pansies, primroses, strawberries, chamomile, cornflowers, and so on. In all, a hundred or so plant species known in the Middle Ages have been identified in these hangings.

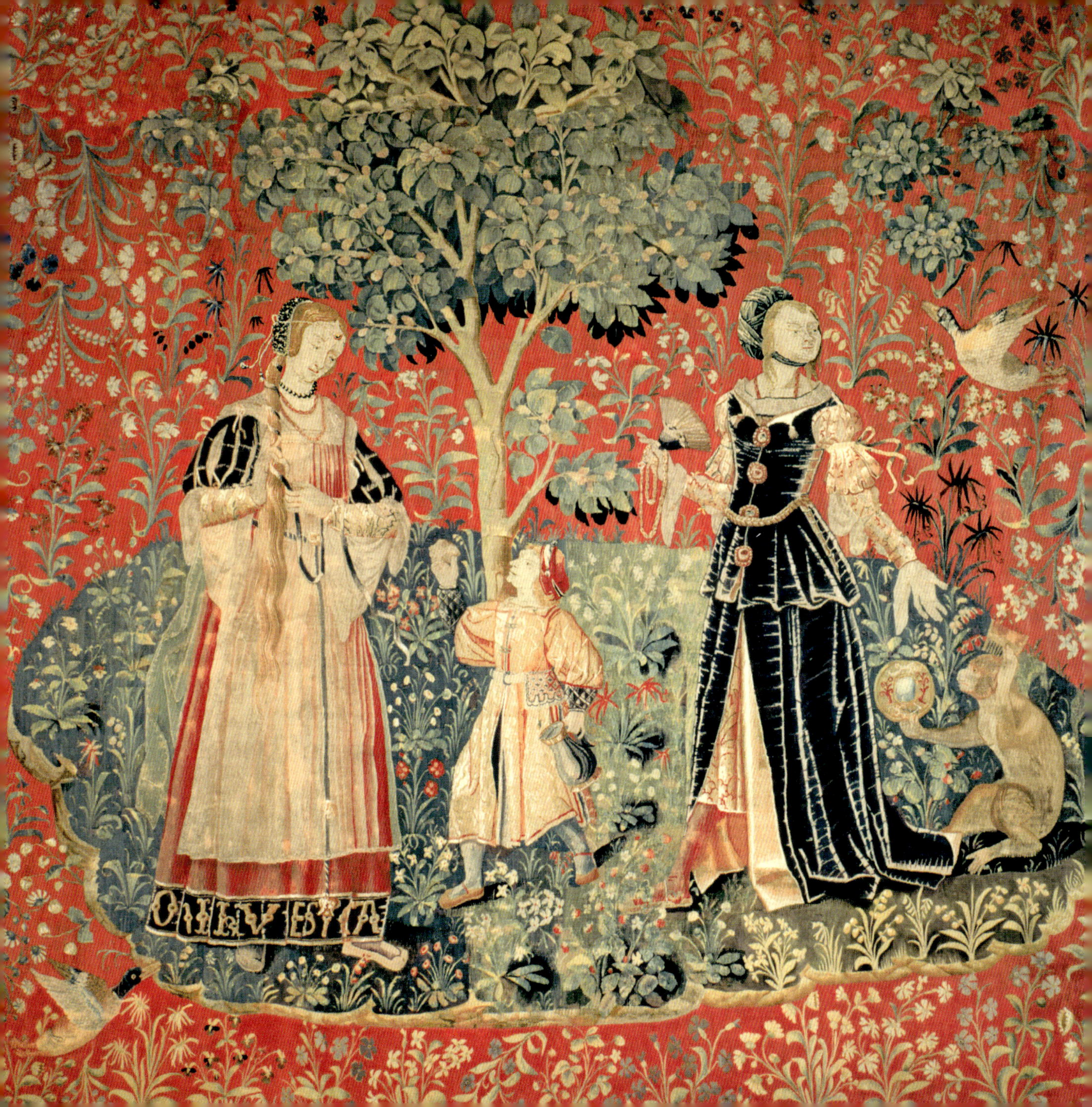
ONKVESYA

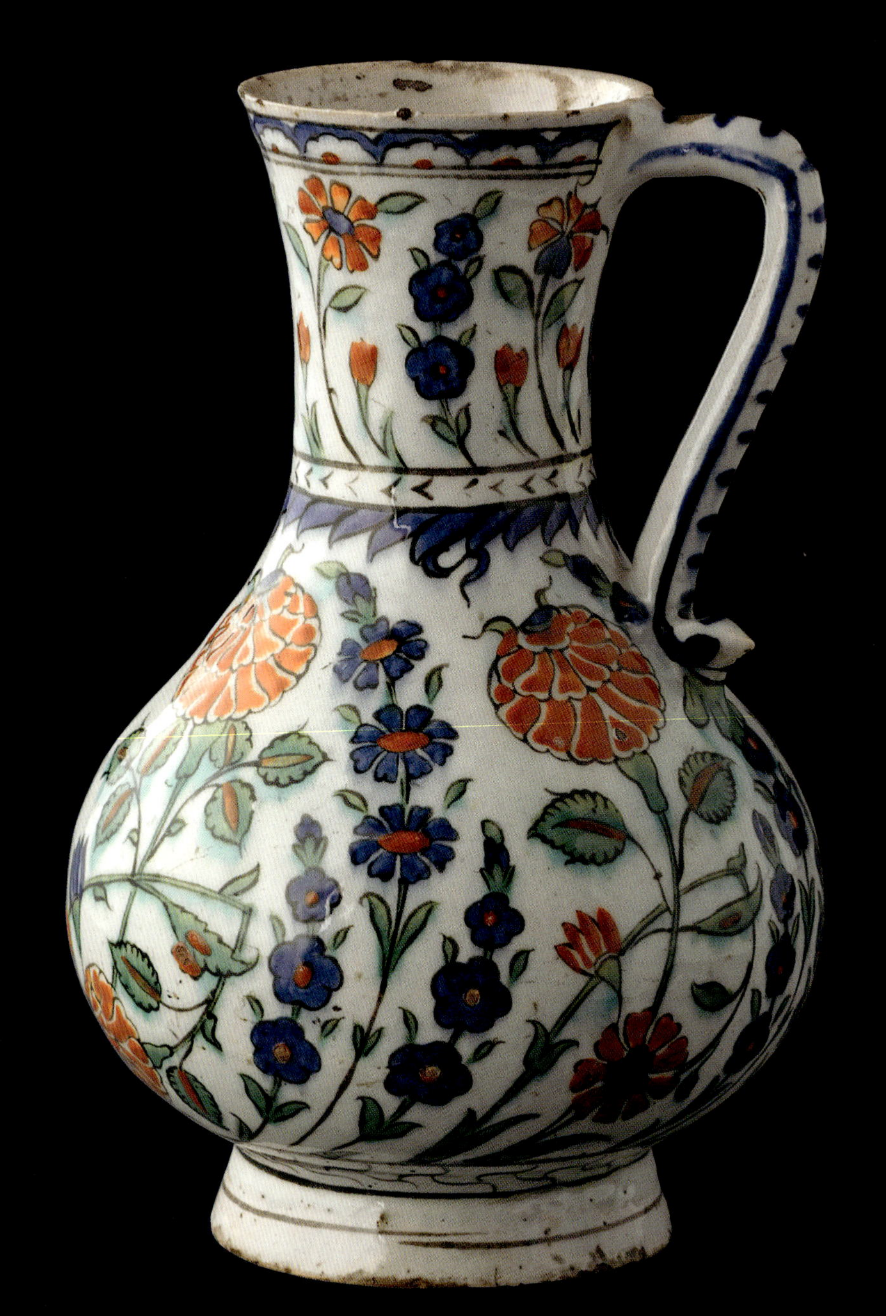

1. **ANONYMOUS**
Pitcher with floral decor
Iznik, Turkey, c. 1560–1570
Quartz-frit ceramic, slip, glaze, paint

2. **ANONYMOUS**
Dish with decor of swirling flowers
Iznik (Turkey), c. 1540–1555
Quartz-frit ceramic, décor painted under
the slip and the transparent glaze

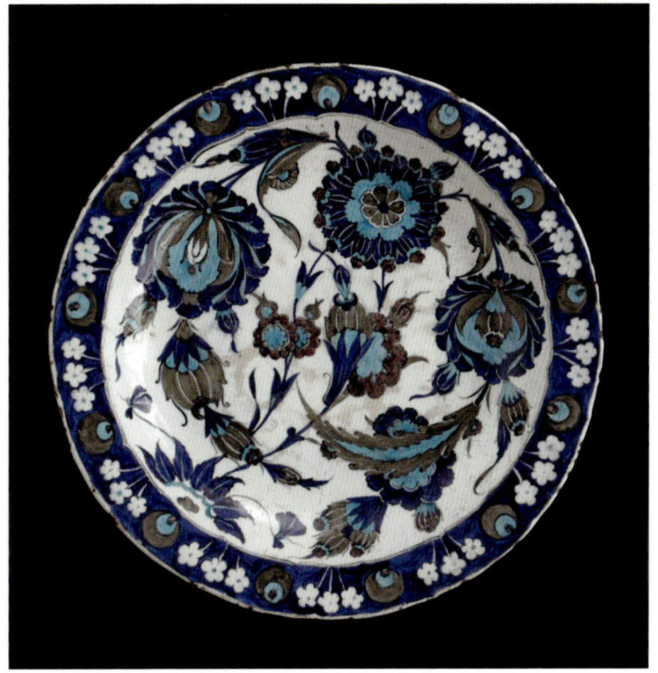

1. Various features of this jug of a form common in the sixteenth century are underlined by its floral decoration. The roses are remarkable for the quality of their dense, brilliant red: appearing in the mid-sixteenth century, this Iznik red became the most highly prized color of all, to the point that it epitomizes the style. So as to avoid empty spaces in the composition and distribute the colors more evenly over the white background, some of the stems from which the roses hang have been snapped. The supple branches laden with blue flowers with red hearts bring out the generous roundness of the vessel's belly to perfection and demonstrate how Iznik potters would arrange their flowers to suit the shape of the vase.

2. Sixteenth-century Western travelers had already noted the interest of the Ottomans in colorful blooms, and the well-watered, temperate climate of Istanbul presented ideal conditions for the gardens planted around the city's countless palaces.

The most frequent motifs on Iznik ceramic pieces are floral ones, and it is conceivable that this was seen as a way of making the gardens of the Ottomans last forever, as flowers are essentially a transitory delight. In 1546, the French traveler Pierre Belon reported that the (ceramic) "craftsmen usually put several flowers of various colors in front of them in a vessel full of water to keep them looking beautiful and fresh." This remark demonstrates how these artists tended to work directly from the model. Iznik potters were masters in using local resources to make ceramics whose gleaming, colorful décor stands out wonderfully against a white ground.

GIUSEPPE ARCIMBOLDO (1527–1593)
Spring, c. 1573
Oil on canvas, 30 x 25 in. (76 x 63.5 cm)

Lily of the valley for the teeth, a peony for the ear, and a white lily on the bonnet in place of a feather. More than eighty kinds of plants with different flowers combine to form the head and upper body of this bust of Spring. Without question Arcimboldo's most famous works are his composite heads made up of disparate but interconnected elements in which clearly identifiable objects are arranged in the shape of the head and shoulders of a bizarre figure.

Hailing originally from Milan, the painter had started working at the imperial court of the Habsburgs in the 1560s, going on to serve three successive emperors: Ferdinand I, Maximilian II, and Rudolf II. In the sixteenth century, the enthusiasm for nature found many different outlets: molding after natural objects, as practiced by Bernard Palissy; realistic engraved plates scientifically depicting plants and animals from the New World; "cabinets of curiosities" housing *naturalia*—natural objects, and their corollary—*artificialia,* the handiwork of man. In the minds of the period, however, some objects belonged strictly speaking to neither category, but were half-natural and half-man-made. In these princely *Kunstkammern,* the relationship between the world of nature and the world of art was epitomized in pieces made of unusual natural materials (ostrich eggs, shells, coral), reworked or mounted into objects to be displayed rather than used.

Arcimboldo was closely involved in the world of the *Kunstkammer* since he had been appointed to select items for the one belonging to the Emperor Rudolf II, and his celebrated series of the *Seasons* is tributary of the unusual context of the cabinet of curiosities in which hybrid forms could arise from the conjunction of nature and art.

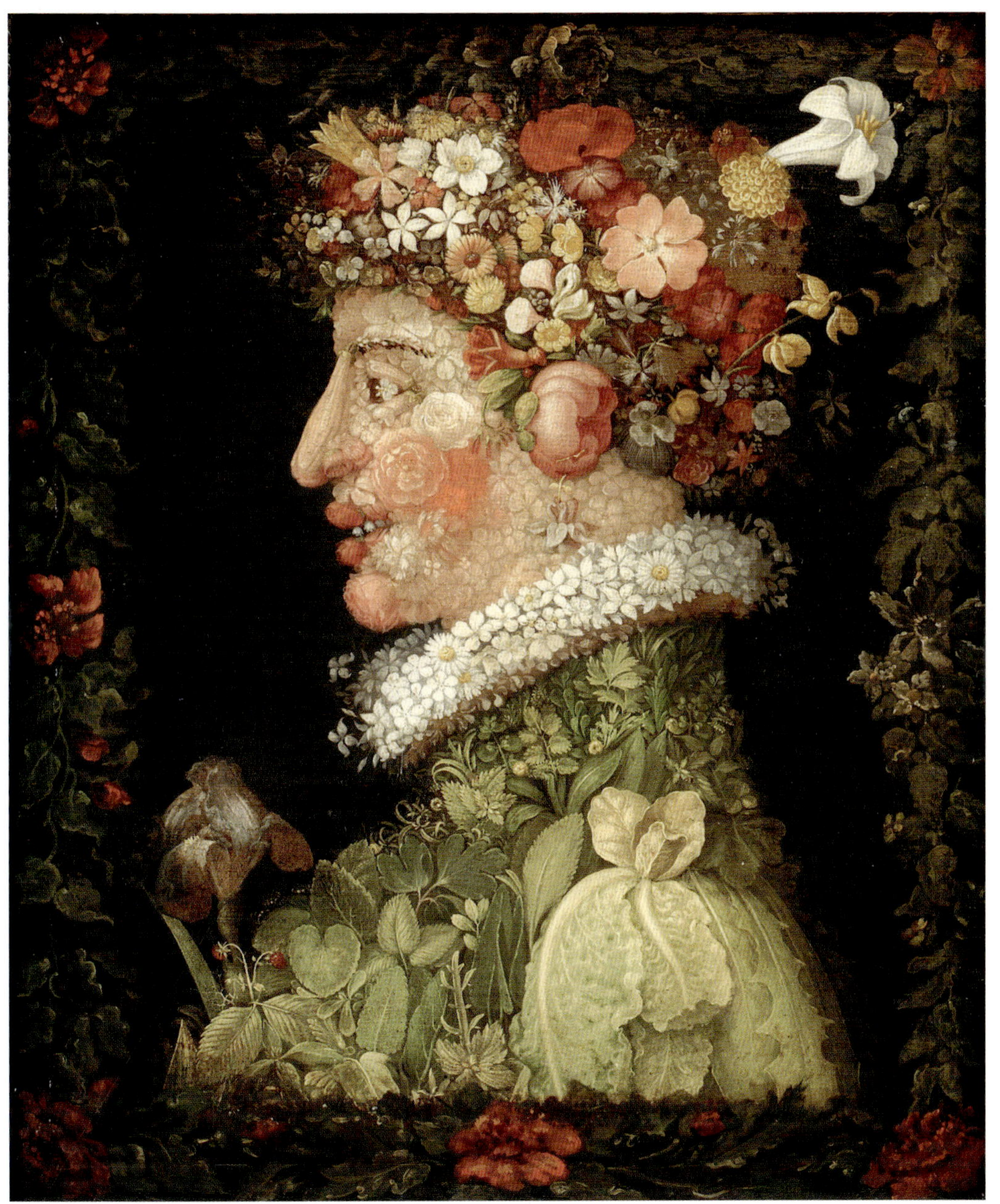

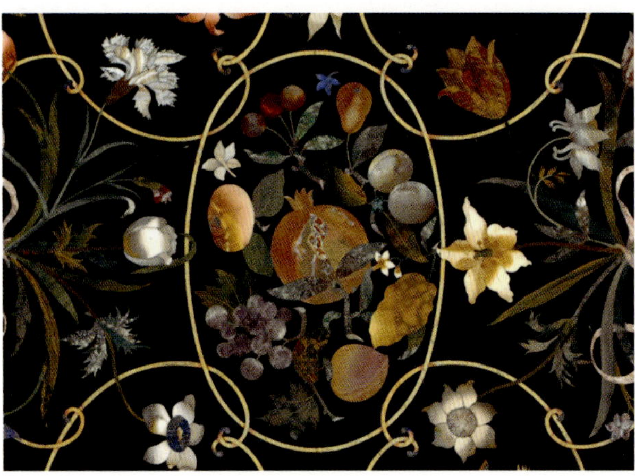

Practiced since Antiquity, the technique of hardstone inlay underwent a notable revival in the mid-sixteenth century, mainly in Rome and Florence, where the Medici founded a prestigious manufacture in 1588. Florentine artists capitalized on the natural colors of hundreds of stones that they cut into wafer-thin slices: malachite, jasper, lapis lazuli, chalcedony, onyx, agate, etc., all play their part in the variegated palette of these marvelous mosaics. The products of this luxury and costly craft remained of course the preserve of princes and popes. The geometrical motifs of the sixteenth century tended to be replaced in the seventeenth by naturalistic depictions of birds and flowers. Age-old stones exhumed from the bowels of the earth were thus transformed into colorful, delicate paintings of fruits, birds, and flowers. On this Florentine tabletop, carnations, narcissi, tulips, and anemones vie for attention in graceful bouquets emerging from the exquisite tracery that offers an elegant echo of the ribbons tying together their stems. It is as if nature has been petrified by a magic spell and imprinted onto a piece of jet-black marble.

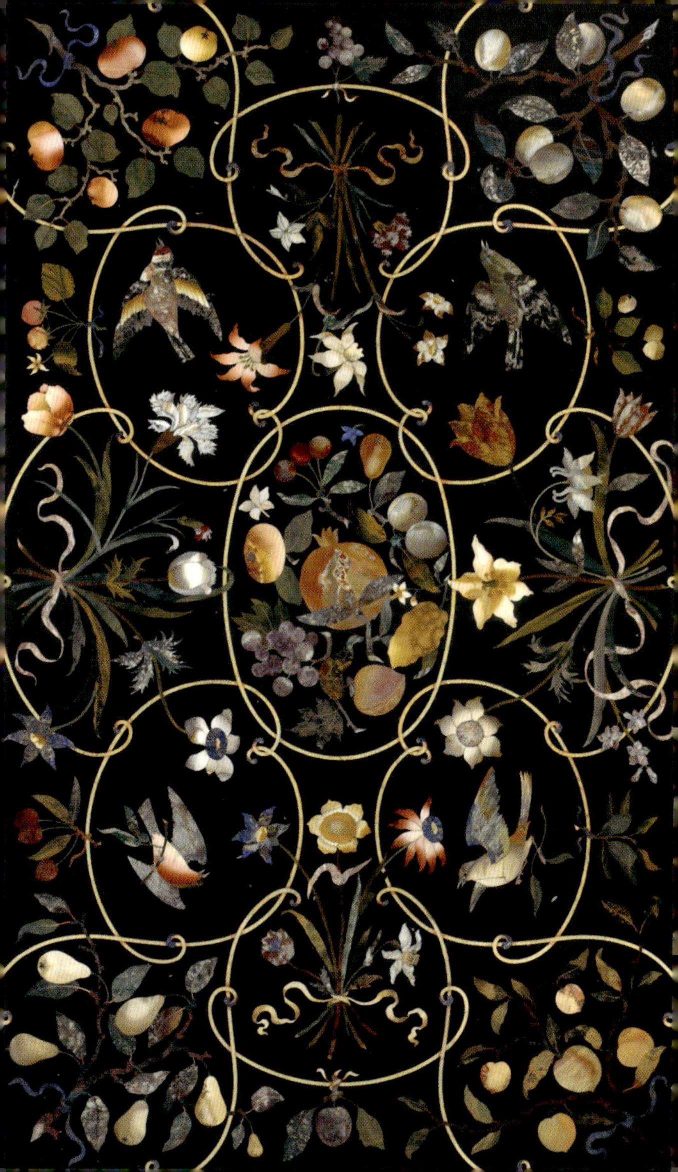

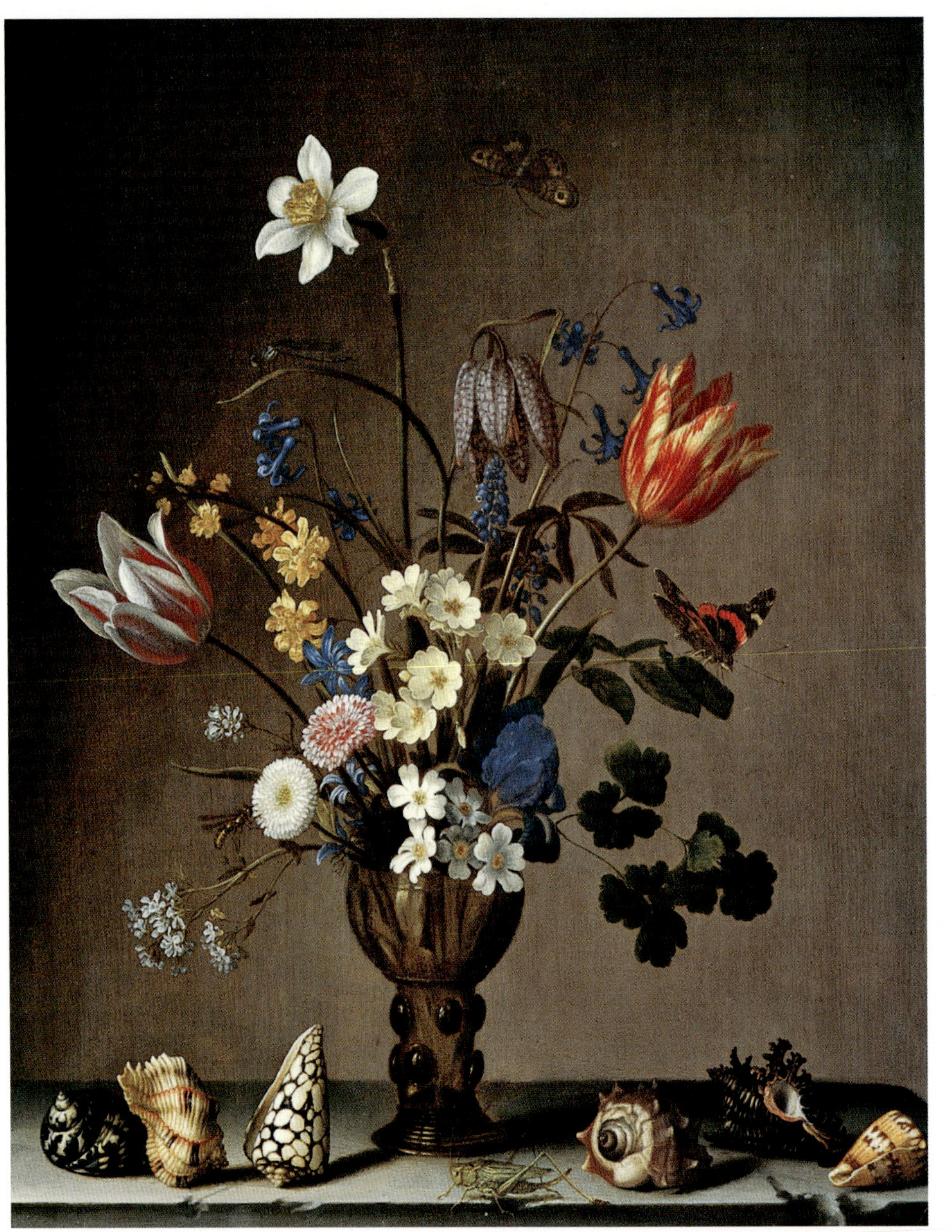

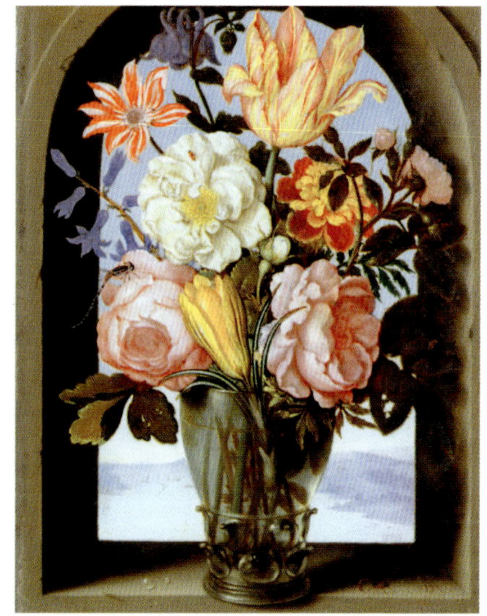

1. **BALTHASAR VAN DER AST** (1593/1594–1657)
Flowers, Shells, Butterflies, and Grasshoppers, c. 1640–1650
Oil on wood, 20 ½ x 16 ½ in. (52 x 42 cm)

2. **AMBROSIUS BOSSCHAERT** (1573–1621)
Bouquet of Flowers in a Stone Arch Opening onto a Landscape, c. 1619–1621
Oil on copper, 9 x 6 ¾ in. (23 x 17 cm)

1. Though it may appear simple, this bouquet conceals a trenchant critique of human vanity.

The arrangement is dominated by the narcissus, an archetype of self-regard and egocentrism. The flower is named for a handsome young man whose story Ovid tells in *Metamorphoses*: rejecting the advances of the nymph, Echo, he would spend his time gazing desperately at his reflection in a pond. Soon wasting away, he expired, and on the site there sprouted the flower that bears his name.

The history of the tulip also epitomizes vanity. Its name has roots in the Turkish "*tülbend*" ("bonnet"), from which the word "turban" also derives. The flower was much prized in Turkey and was introduced in Europe at the end of the 1550s through the Austrian ambassador at Constantinople. In 1593, Charles de l'Écluse, who had observed the blooms in gardens belonging to the emperor of Austria, was appointed professor at Leyden and took his collections with him, thereby sparking the cultivation of the tulip in Holland. Soon the country was in the grip of a veritable craze, known as "tulipomania," as the flowers fell prey to speculation. More than one trader lost his entire fortune buying and selling bulbs that could sometimes attain prices three times that of a Rembrandt. The concern of the government was such that in 1637 it issued a decree forbidding the sale of the wretched bulbs. The flower remained a symbol of the vanity of fame and lemming-like stupidity, and, for this reason, takes pride of place in many floral vanities.

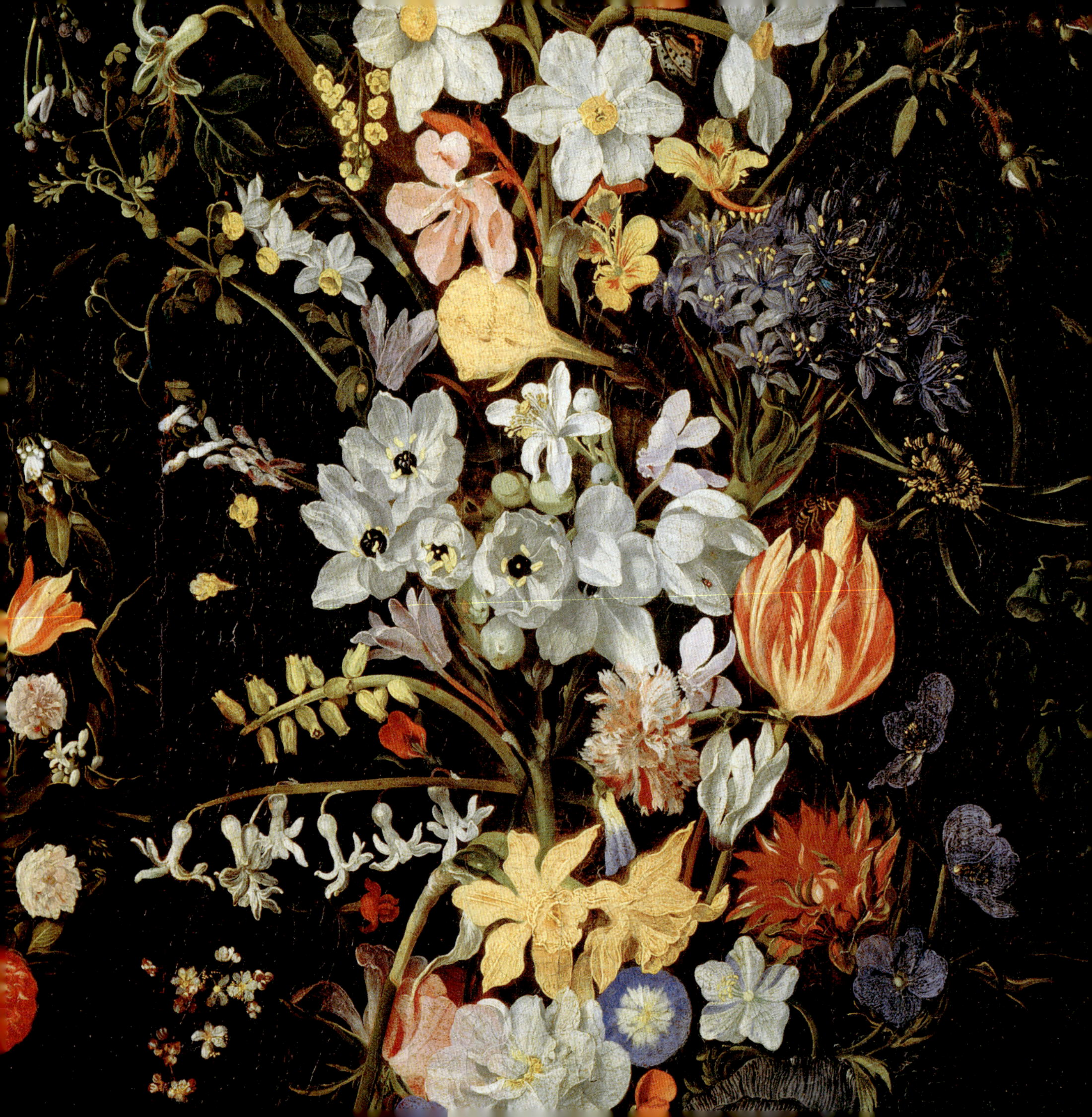

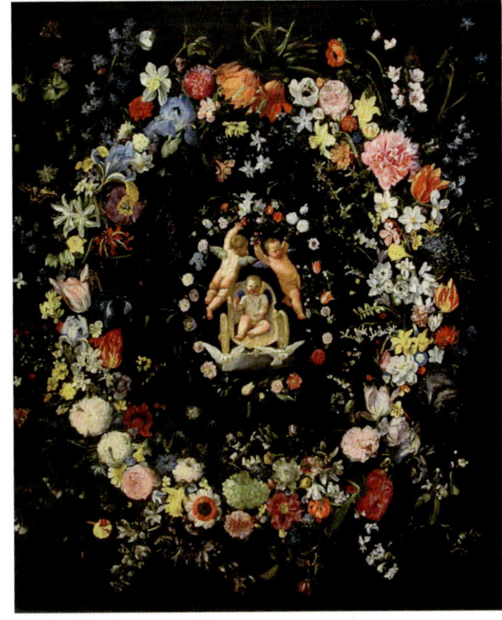

DOMENICO ZAMPIERI, *KNOWN AS* DOMENICHINO (1581–1641)
DANIEL SEGHERS (1590–1661)
The Triumph of Love in a Frame of Flowers, c. 1625–1627
Oil on canvas, 4 ft. 4 ¾ in. x 3 ft. 7 ¼ in. (1.34 x 1.10 m)

Flowers can speak of love and it would seem that Ludovico Ludovisi, one of the pope's nephews, was intent on illustrating this fact when he commissioned Domenichino to add three winged putti—one of whom is enthroned on a chariot drawn by two doves—to a floral garland the Jesuit painter Daniel Seghers had presented him with several years previously. The artist dubbed "the painter of flowers and the flower of painters" had made a specialty of floral crowns or wreaths, which, because Seghers belonged to the Order of the Jesuits, were not intended for sale, but to decorate churches or as gifts for people of rank. The majority of these flower pieces were completed by some other artist with a picture in the middle on a sacred theme. In fact, this garland symbolizes the garden generally, in an echo of the medieval *hortus conclusus* or walled garden, which, in the *Song of Songs*, prefigures Mary's virginity. It is not intended, though, that we hunt down an inherent symbolic role for every last species in this tumbling, teeming mass of tulips, roses, irises, hyacinths, and bindweed: all this floral bounty speaks simply of broader ideals of purity, love, fertility, abundance, and virtue, offering a sufficiently all-embracing vision to allow it to pass relatively smoothly from the religious to the profane sphere.

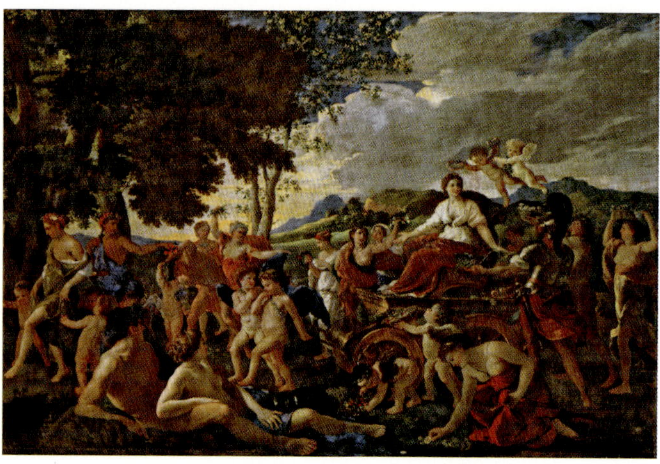

Seated on her chariot, Flora, goddess of spring, dominates the composition, accompanying various mortals who have been transformed into flowers by divine edict. Viewed from the rear, Ajax, laden with armor and helmet, brings her flowers on his shield. This hero of the Trojan War had committed suicide by throwing himself on his sword in fury because he had been refused the weapons of Achilles. The ground reddened by his blood gave birth to a crimson flower. Half hidden behind Ajax, Narcissus can be seen presenting his blooms to the goddess in a basket. Kneeling in the foreground, Clytia picks a heliotrope: in love with Apollo, she was metamorphosed into that flower, which turns its head as it follows the god's incarnation, the sun. At the head of the procession, Venus, trying out a dance step, is followed by Adonis carrying a lance. When Adonis was fatally wounded by a wild boar, anemones sprouted from his blood. He holds out a bunch to Hyacinthus, a young boy with whom Apollo had fallen in love only to kill him accidentally at a discus competition, transforming him into the flower that bears his name, the hyacinth.

These floral references are in fact all famous episodes from *Metamorphoses*, though the scene shown here does not illustrate any specific passage in Ovid's poem. Poussin is not an illustrator and ventures a personal reading of the myths. In spite of the tragic destinies of the various lovers in his picture, the artist has created a luminous, shimmering canvas, an allegory of the eternal rebirth of spring.

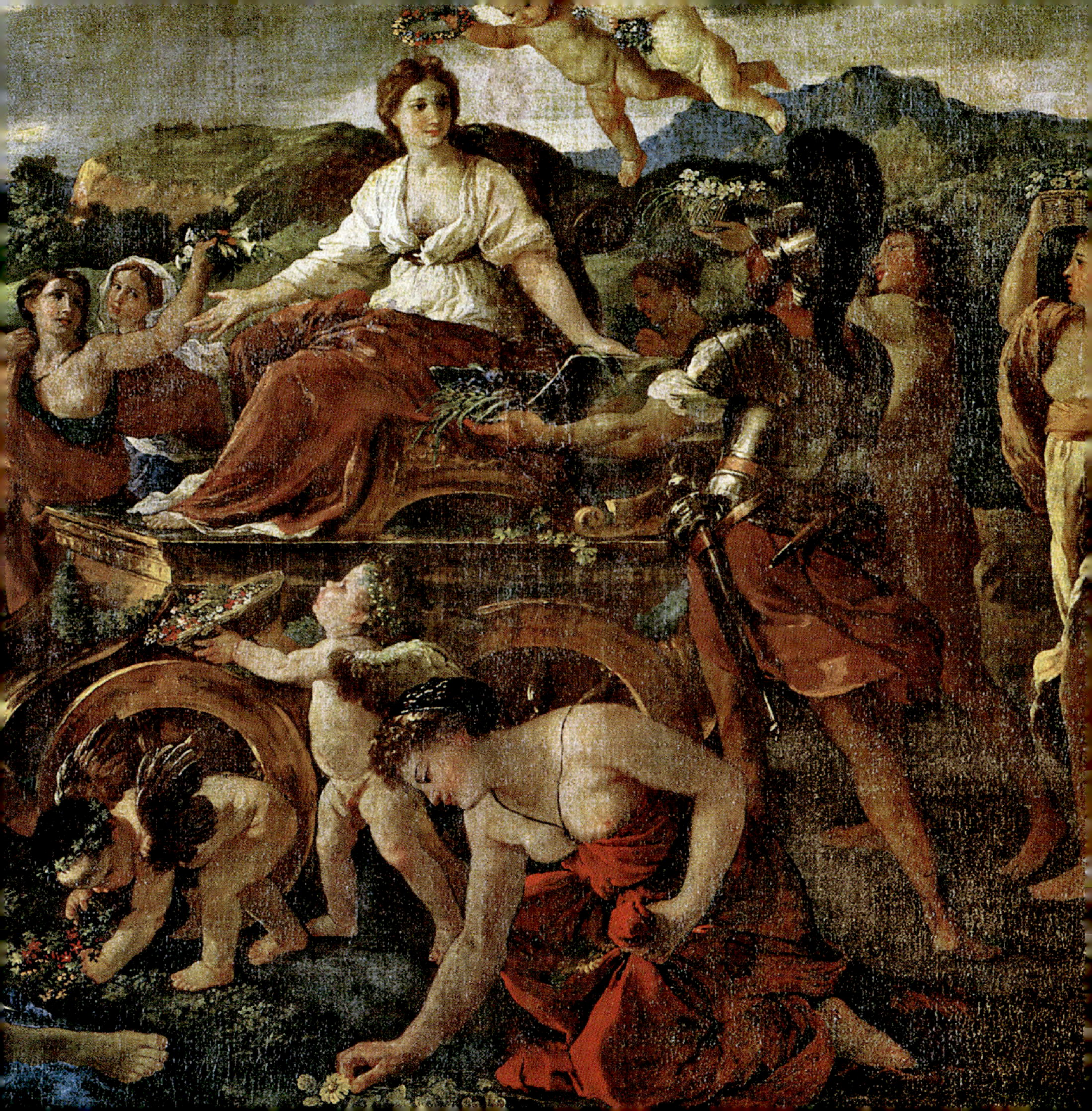

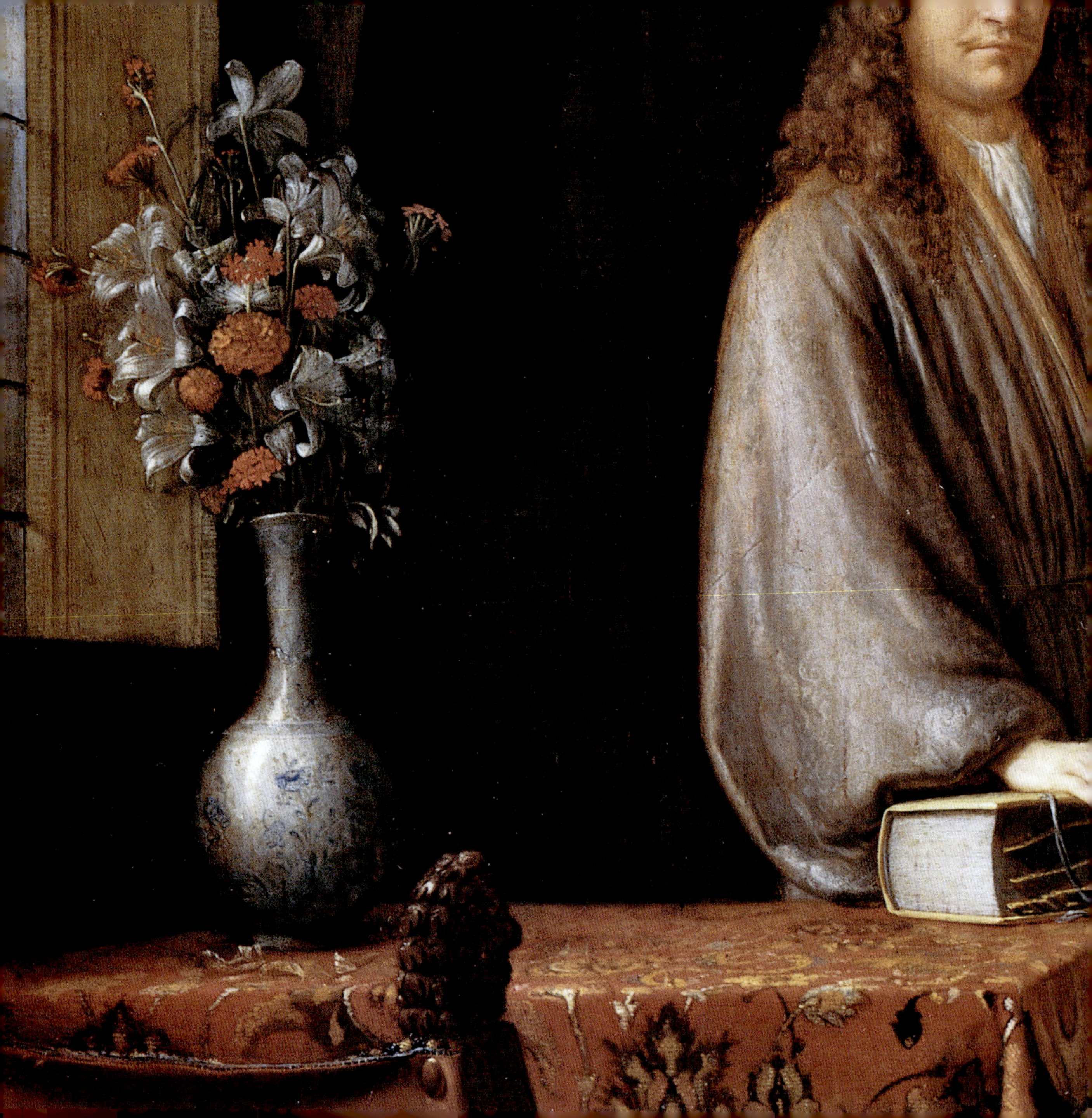

PIETER CORNELISZ VAN SLINGELANDT
(c. 1625/1630–1691)
*Frans Meerman, Scrivener of the City
of Leyden with his Family,* 1668
Oil on wood, 20 ¾ x 17 ¼ in. (53 x 44 cm)

In a vast hall, furnished sparsely but with
pieces of high quality, five figures pose
before the painter. To the right, on the
table draped in a splendid carpet, a very
simple bunch of flowers shows itself to
best advantage in a white porcelain vase
with a blue floral pattern. The white lilies
and orange carnations seem to have been
arranged rather haphazardly. In spite
of its name, the "French" (or "pot")
marigold is a species that originated
in Mexico, being introduced into Europe
in 1573. Like the lily, it became an
allegorical attribute of the sense of smell.
Unlike the opulent floral pieces common
in Dutch painting in this era, which
mixed flowers from various seasons,
the two species shown here both flower
in July, making the bouquet a plausible
composition, in agreement with the
overall realism of the scene.

It would probably be unwise though
to look for much symbolism in these
painstakingly delineated flowers, as their
attraction for the painter derives
essentially from their delicate coloring
and glorious finish. A tentative allusion
to the natural world, they form a colorful
counterpoint to the cloth on the table,
the stage curtain thrown back to reveal

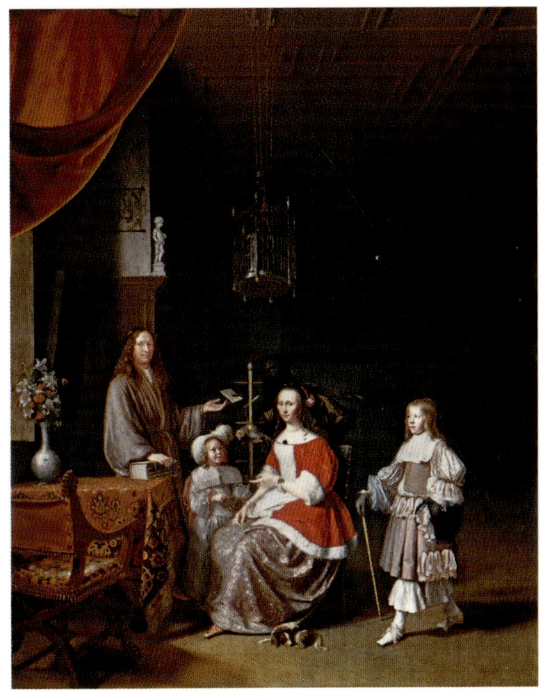

the scene, and the opulent ermine-
trimmed scarlet coat of velvet worn by
the lady of the house. Jean-Baptiste
Descamps tells us that the artist would
spend three years on painting a square
foot of canvas and took no less than
a month to do the lace lappet sported
by the young man. For Slingelandt's
microscopic approach to painting,
a few lilies and a spray of pinks amount
to a full-scale garden!

In this skillfully composed piece, the bright colors of a few flowers of the field mingling with some grass stems stand out at the foot of great oak looming out of the dark undergrowth. The eye is initially drawn to the glowing red poppy that droops on its frail stalk. Its name in French, *coquelicot,* derives from *cocorico,* the onomatopoeic equivalent of the English "cock-a-doodle-doo," due to its resemblance to the color of a rooster's "cockscomb." Like poppies, cornflowers used to thrive in wheat fields before they were practically eradicated by modern agriculture and its chemicals. The poppy was believed to be an effective antidote against snake bites, a reassuring thought as one of the animals crawling about possesses a none-too friendly air! The daisy too is a flower of grassy slopes, and who has not at some point pulled off its petals asking the all-important question: "She loves me? she loves me not? she loves me?"

If at the end of the nineteenth century these three wild flowers were often associated with the French tricolor and patriotic compositions, two centuries earlier Abraham Mignon would have combined them for different reasons: since it can flower almost anywhere, the daisy had become a symbol of the love of the Virgin Mary that triumphs over all, while the poppy evokes Christ's sacrifice, and the cornflower purity of spirit. The message is further underlined by the animals chosen: close to the ground, the reptiles recall a material world that is fated to one day disappear, while the butterflies and birds, on the other hand, flying up in the sky, express the soul that lives on forever after the body perishes.

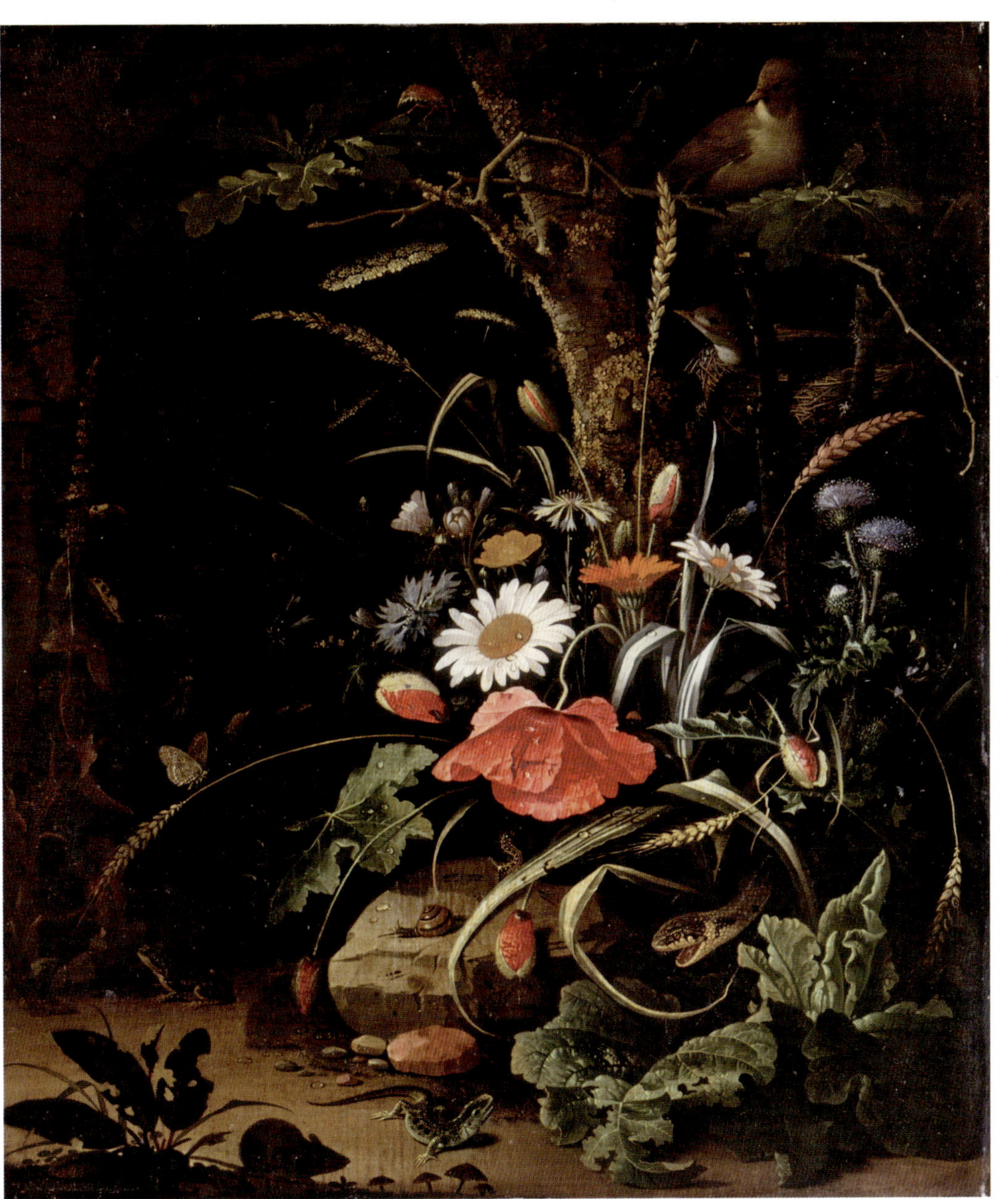

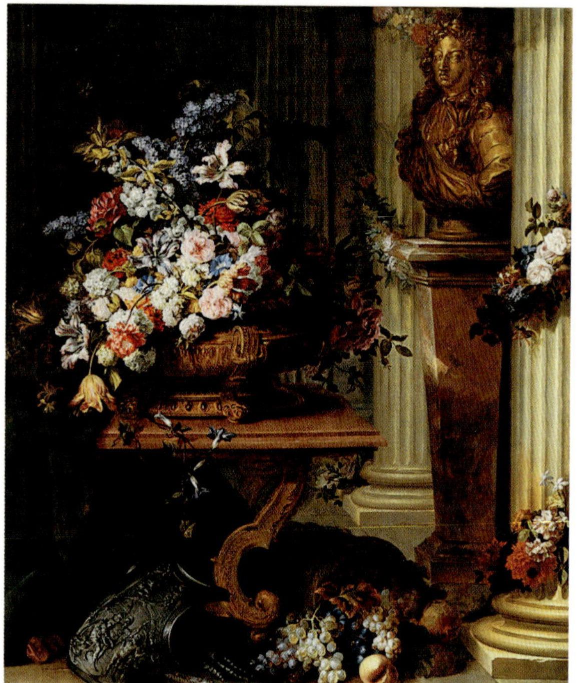

JEAN BELIN, *CALLED* BLAIN DE FONTENAY
(1653–1715)
*Flowers in a Gold Vase, Bust of Louis XIV,
Horn of Plenty and Armor*, 1687
Oil on canvas, 6 ft. 2 ¾ in. x 5 ft. 3 ¾ in.
(1.9 x 1.62 m)

For his reception piece into the French Academy of Painting in 1687, Jean Blain de Fontenay painted the perspective view of an impressive colonnade in whose shadow explodes a sumptuous bunch of peonies, carnations, tulips, and divers roses looking like a firework display. The king, guardian of the arts, is present in the form of a portrait bust, a clearly valuable piece whose golden shimmer vies with the dazzling, wonderfully fresh bouquet.

The discarded suit of armor and the horn of plenty overflowing with fruit are, like the flowers scattered over the composition, tributes to a victorious yet peace-loving monarch. The profusion of flowers that here mingles with the spread of luxury is a far cry from the elegant geometry of the French-style gardens that were the rule in the age of Louis XIV. The point here is to show that the absolutism of the sovereign extends to all he surveys, both in the human and the natural worlds.

If the painter keeps faith with the delicate brushwork of the Dutch, he does not paint flowers for themselves, but amplifies the decorative impact by emphasizing the effect of the masses in their space: this spread of flowers—hovering between light and shade— is as monumental as any of Le Brun's human heroes.

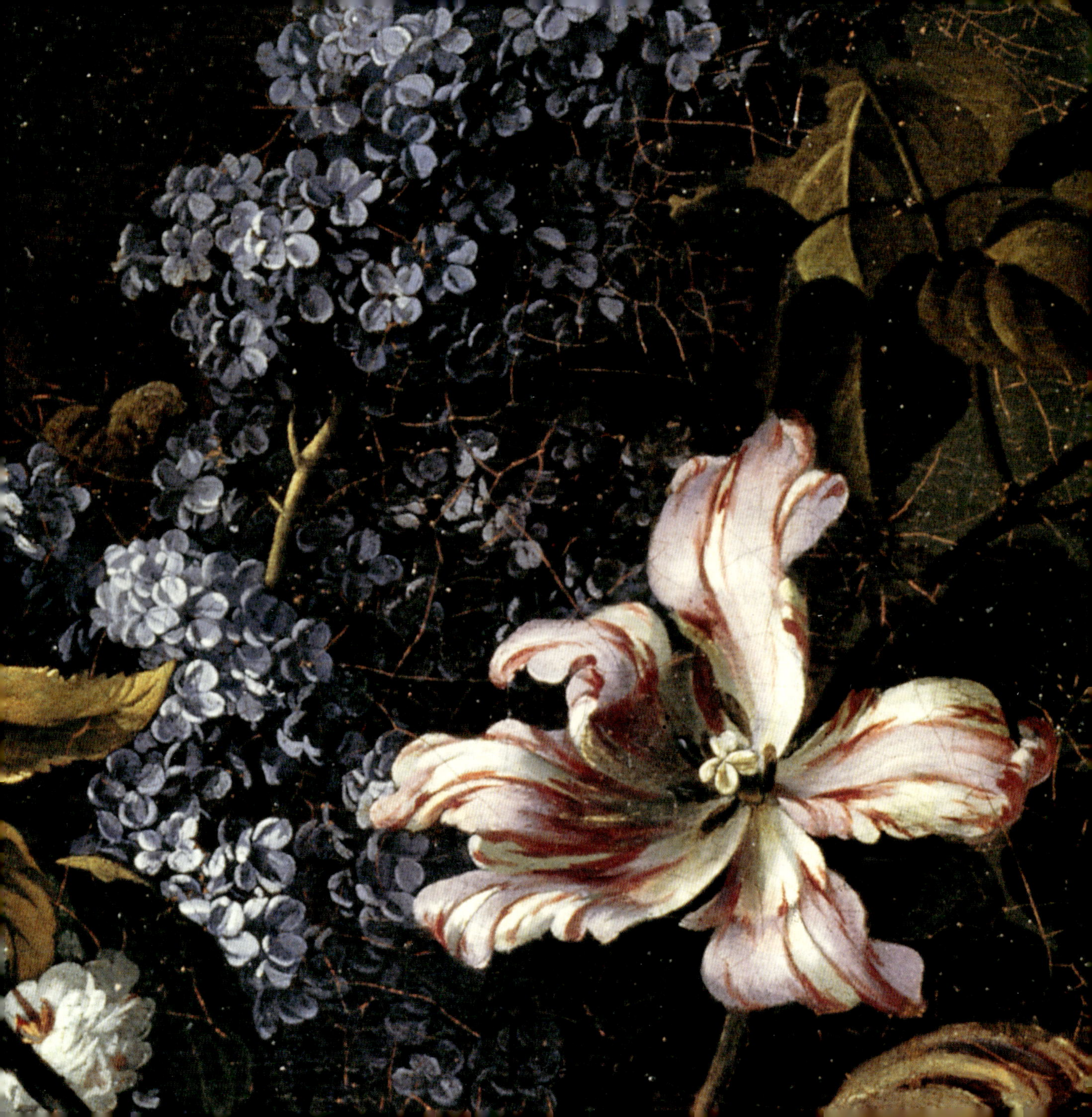

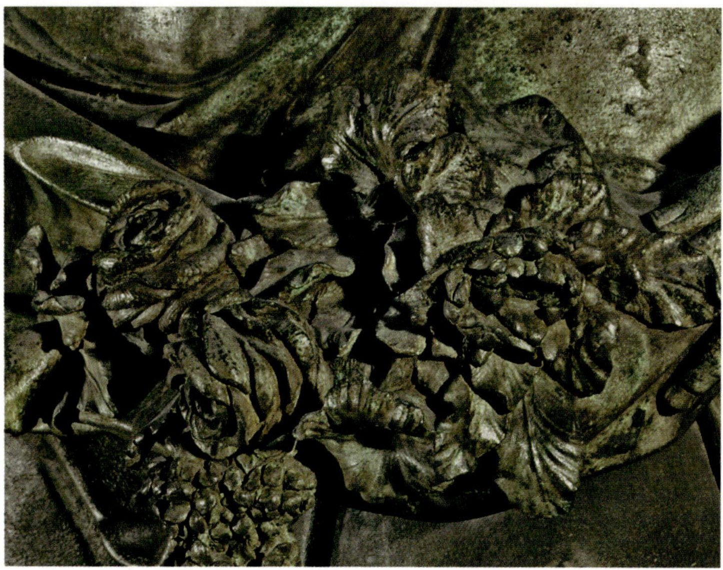

AFTER **FRANÇOIS GIRARDON** (1628–1715),
JEAN-BALTHAZAR KELLER (CASTER) (1638–1702), **PHILIPPE MAGNIER** (1648–1715)
Aurora, c. 1686–1694
Bronze, 6 ft. 8 ¾ in. x 4 ft. 1 ¼ in. x 3 ft. 7 ¾ in. (2.05 x 1.25 x 1.11 m)

Due to the sheer quantity of flowers it features, this sculpture representing the goddess Aurora, which once graced the park in the Château de Marly, is also sometimes called *Flora*. That goddess married the West Wind, Zephyr, in May, receiving as her wedding gift dominion over the world of flowers. Zephyr seems to be living up to his name as his breath flattens the tunic to her body and puffs out the drapery in ample billows.

From her chariot in the shape of a shell, the graceful goddess alights and strews rose petals over the ground as an announcement, perhaps, of a new dawn or of the return of spring. *Flora* or *Dawn*, it does not matter which—we can delight in the marvelous chiseling of this rose wreath whoever she is. The skill of the sculptor Jacques Desjardins, responsible for giving it its finishing touches, gloriously captures the intricate, overlapping petals of the flower.

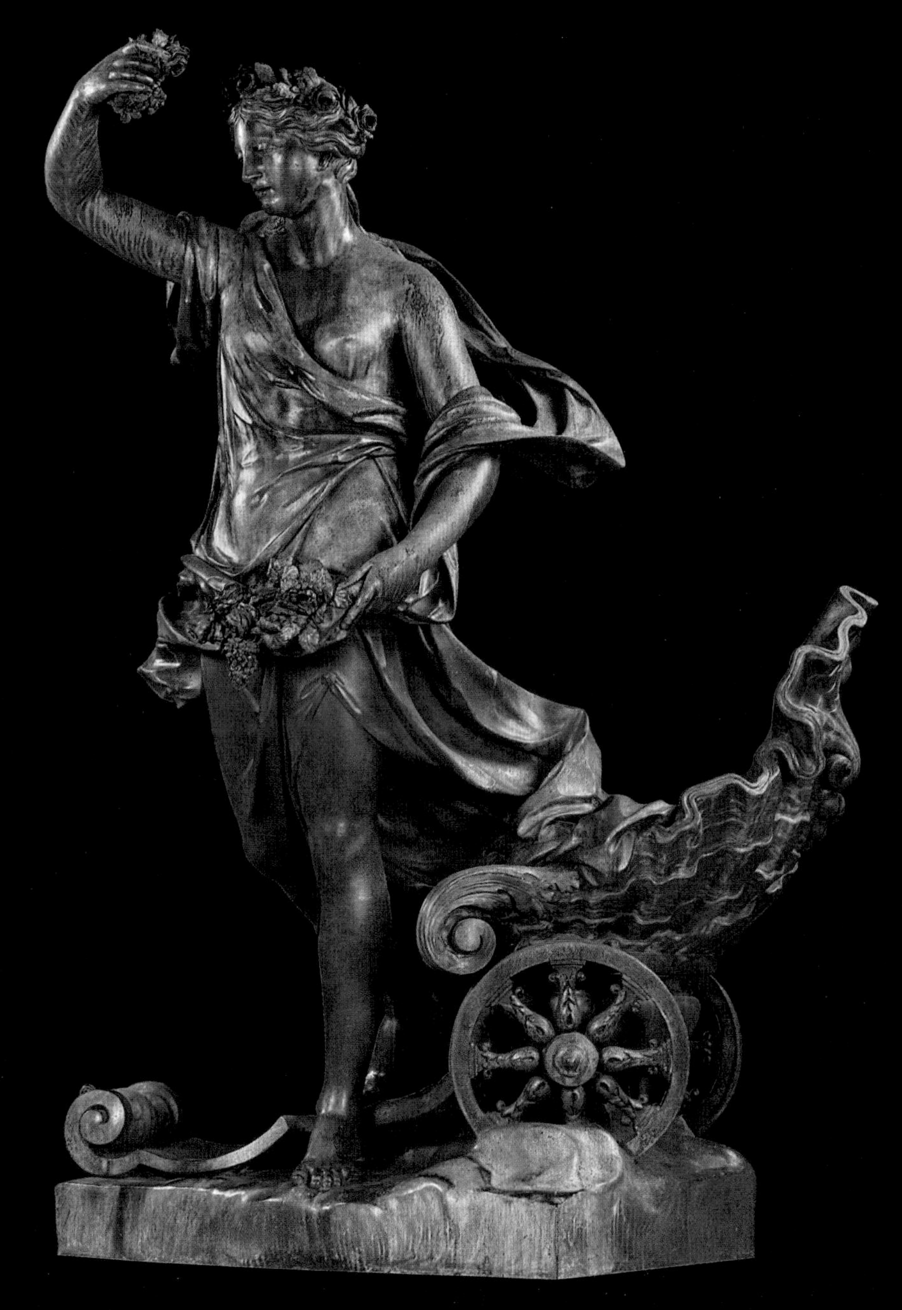

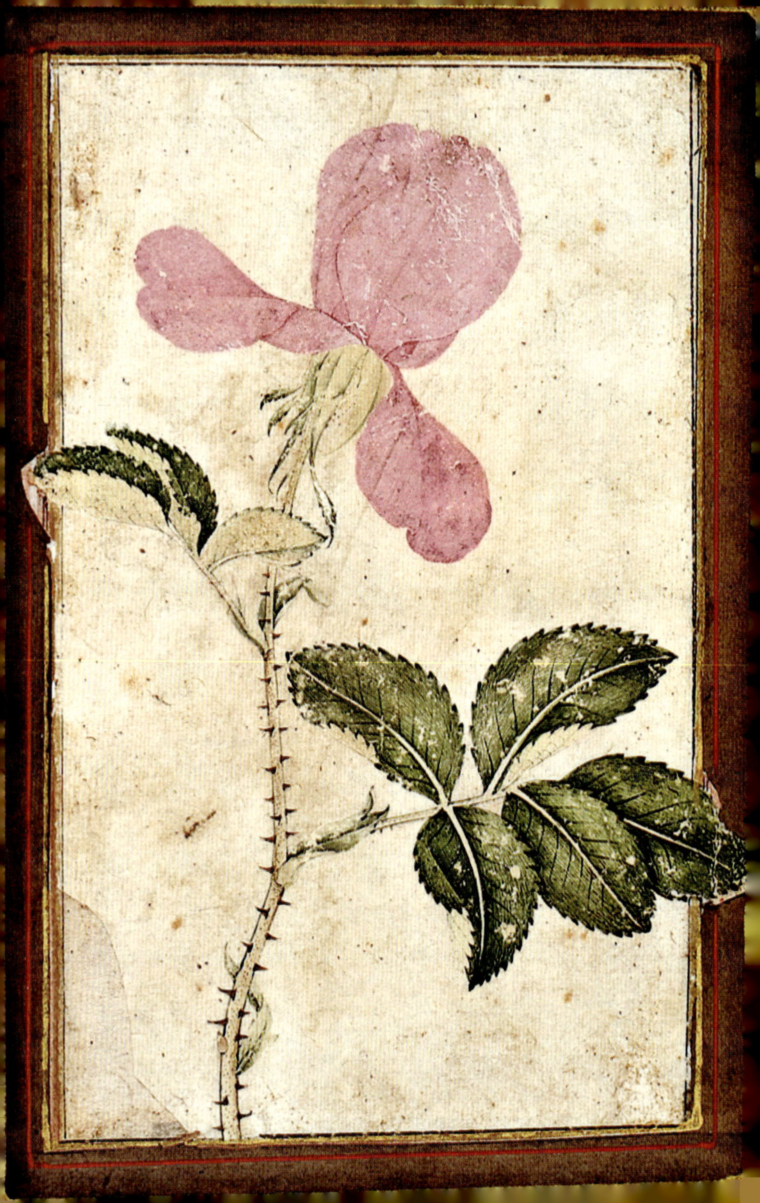

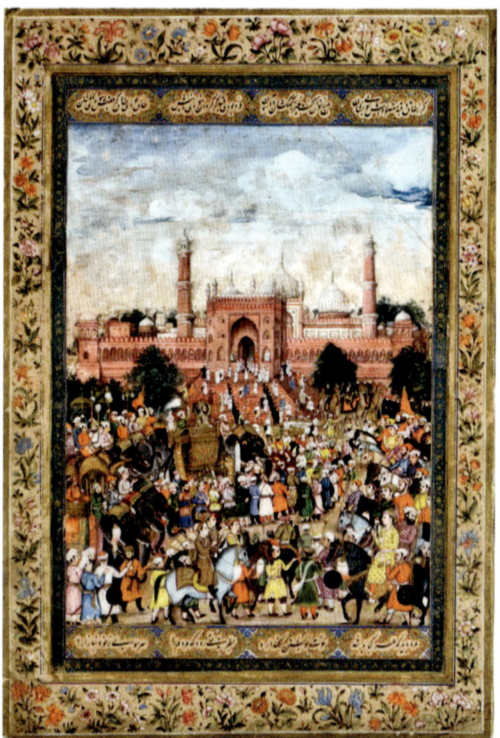

1. At the end of an elongated, spiky stem, a wild-rose bloom opens its delicate pastel-pink petals, flanked on either side of the composition by serrated leaves in various tones of green. The tips of the leaves continue beyond the frame because the miniature has been cut out of the original manuscript and mounted onto a piece of cardboard.

Up until the eighteenth century, depictions of flowers in Persian miniatures were secondary motifs, though in larger compositions they might often be invested with symbolic significance. At the end of the Safavid period, the role of the miniature changed: its function was no longer to illustrate a text and it could now exist quite independently. Thus, under the dual influence of engraved plates from European herbaria and Mughal art, flowers, which had always been a much-loved theme among Iranian artists, were now a painted subject in and for themselves.

Eglantines are wild roses whose botanical name, *Rosa canina* ("dog-rose"), comes from an ancient concoction against rabies made from their roots. Today, the flower symbolizes fleeting joy and brief love affairs.

Even if it is improbable that the artist wanted his drawing to take on such an allegorical meaning, the delicate petals, as if threatened by their thorny stalk, admirably epitomize the poetic fragility of hopeless love.

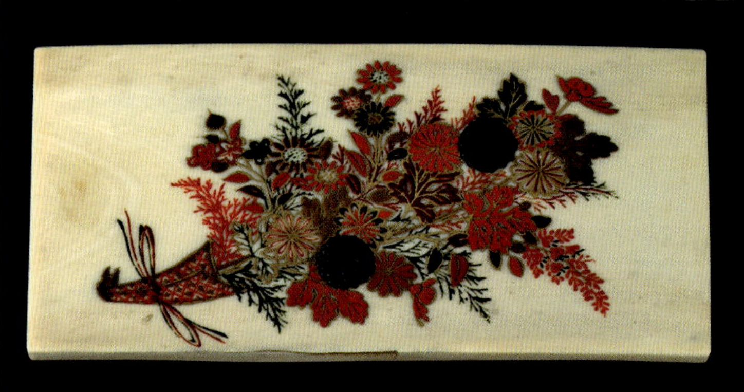

1. ANONYMOUS
Box painted with a bunch of flowers
Japan, n. d.

2. *Fragment of a curtain from the Grand Salon at the Château d'Abondant,* c. 1750
Embroidery, painting on silk,
5 ½ in. (3.7 cm)

1. The paneling and furniture in the drawing room in the Château d'Abondant (Eure-et-Loir) convey an excellent idea of how a French country house would have been decorated in the mid-eighteenth century. As early as the late seventeenth century, the creation of the East India and Levant Companies had introduced many wonders from the Far East, such as textiles, objets d'art, lacquer, and porcelain, to the West.

2. Cabinetmakers and tapestry designers would lift Oriental motifs from their intended context and incorporate them into a language of new forms in the fashionable *rocaille* style. To top off the sophisticated décor in this *salon*, the painted and embroidered silk curtains—without tie-backs and cut from "Peking" fabric adorned with flowers of Chinese inspiration—tumble freely to the floor. The plant species are not easily recognizable since from the same stem ornamented with sawtooth leaves sprout various stylized blooms, vaguely related to roses, dahlias, and perhaps even water irises. In the beginning, "Peking" designated a Chinese silk painted with a kind of gouache. It was the height of fashion in the eighteenth century, in particular in the Marquise de Pompadour's Château de Bellevue. The name, however, did not necessary indicate the place where the textile had been woven, and this particular silk is of Western origin. It has to be admitted though that it is easier for poets than explorers to find their way through the maze of antiquated place-names given to such textiles, since the geographical designations applied to many fabrics and weaves were utterly fanciful.

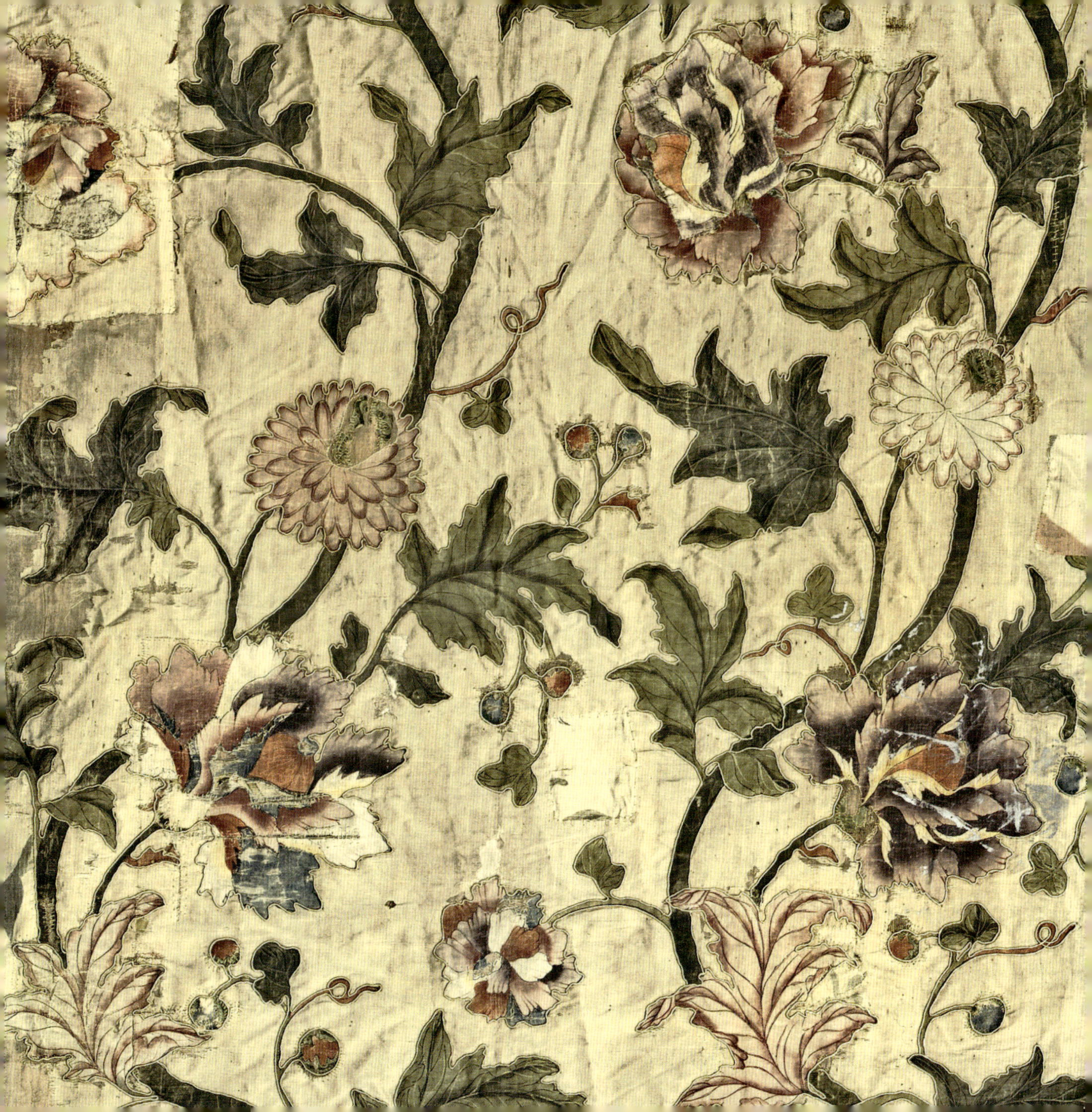

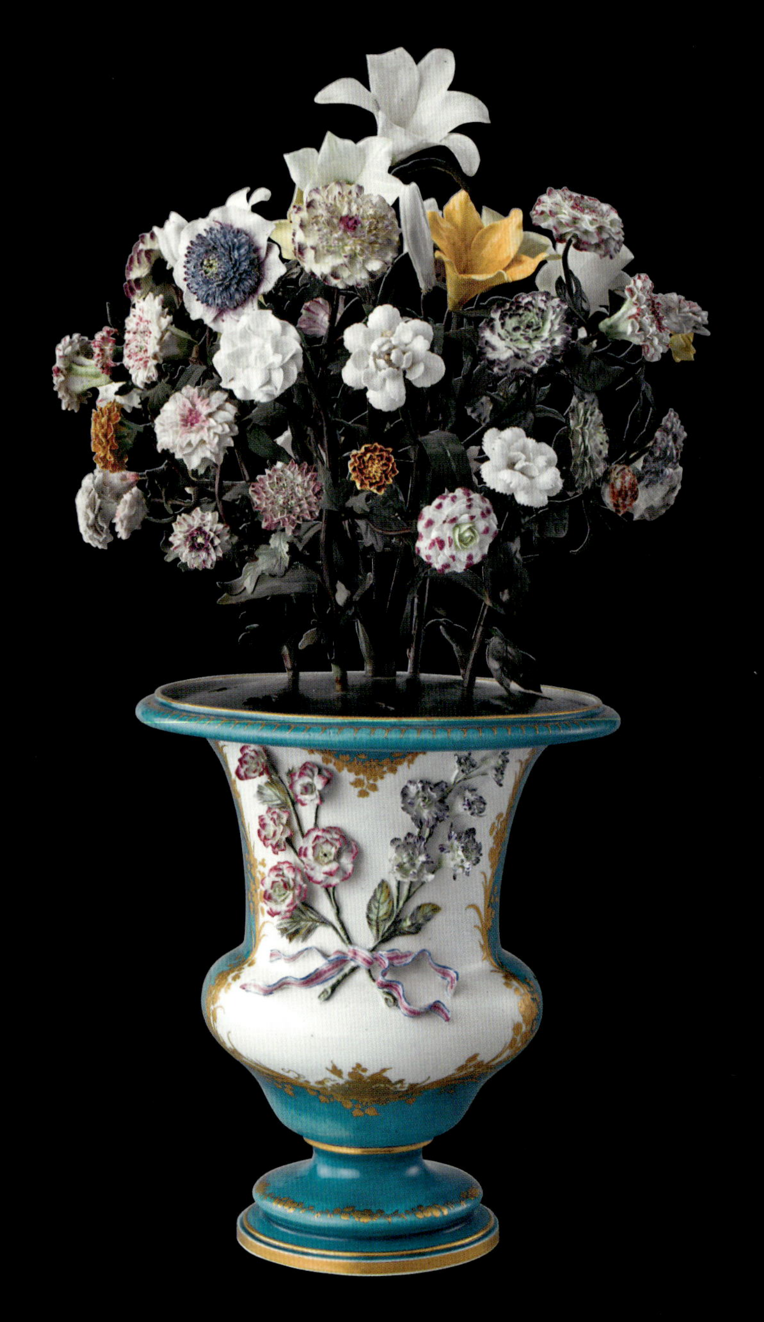

1. VINCENNES MANUFACTURE
"Le Boitteux" Vase, 1755
Soft-paste porcelain, 11 x 9 ½ in. (28 x 24 cm)
(including flowers: 12 ¼ x 13 in. [31 x 33 cm])

2. FRANÇOIS BOUCHER (1703–1770)
Girl Holding a Basket of Flowers, 1756
Pastel on parchment, 17 ¼ x 14 ½ in.
(44 x 37 cm)

1. Madame de Pompadour was more than
just a royal favorite: as regards the fine arts
at court, it was she who ruled the roost.
While the floral fashion was all the rage
in Paris, she visited the porcelain factory
set up by the brothers Dubois, who had
persuaded Orry de Fulvy, a senior member
of the Council of State and minister of
finance, to secure them a room in a tower
at the Château de Vincennes and allot
them a substantial subsidy to kick-start the
French porcelain industry. In about 1741,
the Vincennes Manufacture had
distinguished itself by inventing the floral
design in relief. The basic idea had come
from Meissen, but, instead of incorporating
semi-relief flowers into the decoration
in the Saxon manner, artists in Vincennes
preferred to treat them like genuine flowers
and arrange them into bunches on branches
of lacquered metal. On her visit,
La Pompadour was overjoyed to come
across porcelain flowers enameled and
painted so naturally that they added
dazzling verisimilitude to the obvious
advantage of never wilting. More than

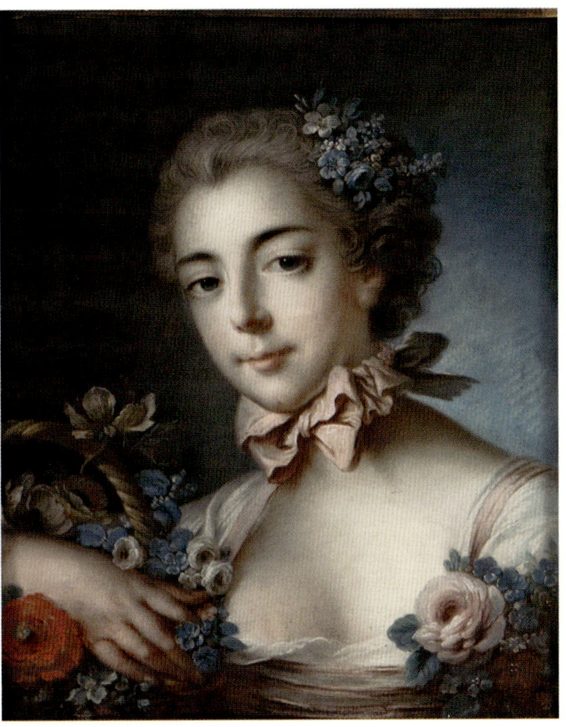

a hundred different species were available
as buds, half open or in full bloom, and
in a wide range of prices from a mere two
sols to a hefty nine *livres*. This Medici-type
vase on a turquoise-blue ground bears
the name of Claude Le Boitteux, a bronze-
founder and -mounter who worked at
the Vincennes Manufacture. It presents
not only a bouquet in the French style but
also a relief floral décor shaped into a spray
held together by a typically Saxon ribbon.

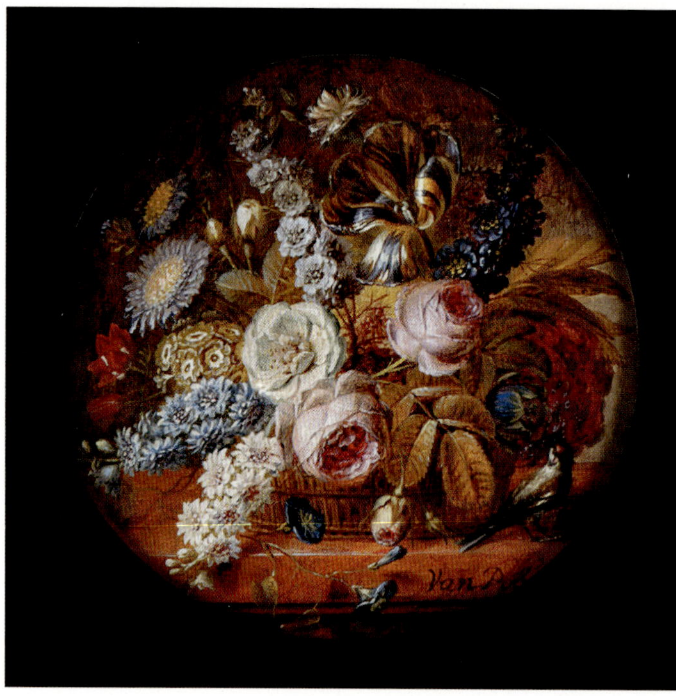

2. Several blooms among this sizable bunch seem to be drooping or withering. The occasional stem has snapped under the sheer weight of the corolla, while others are leaning over dangerously. The central group of peonies, roses, narcissi, tuberose, and white tulip forms a light-colored clump surrounded by foliage and by the less exuberant hues of tulips, violets, hyacinths, irises, and bear's ears (primroses). As if left to its own devices, this bouquet has definitely seen better days and has lost all cohesion. No one has bothered to straighten it out and rearrange the composition a bit more symmetrically.

Van Dael here remains faithful to the codes of the autonomous flower genre created two centuries before in Holland: the vase stands on a shelf with butterflies fluttering around it. But while painters of earlier centuries sought to make a moral point by arranging the flowers in accordance with a symbolic system in which each species had a special meaning, here the artist adapts the message to nineteenth-century taste. Busier in his details, he delineates each branch so as to make this costly looking bouquet still more tangible and material. Such descriptive virtuosity is a perfect expression of the scientific objectivity of the period that was related to a renewed interest in the now autonomous science of botany, which, at the end of the eighteenth century, had at long last broken free from medicine to become an independent and popular discipline.

1. **CHRISTIAEN VAN POL** (1752–1813)
*Vase adorned with bas-relief
and decorated with flowers*
Miniature on enamel, 3 x 3 in. (7.5 x 7.5 cm)

2. **JAN FRANS VAN DAEL** (1764–1840)
Vase of Flowers, Grapes, and Peaches, 1810
Oil on canvas, 39 x 31 in. (99 x 79 cm)

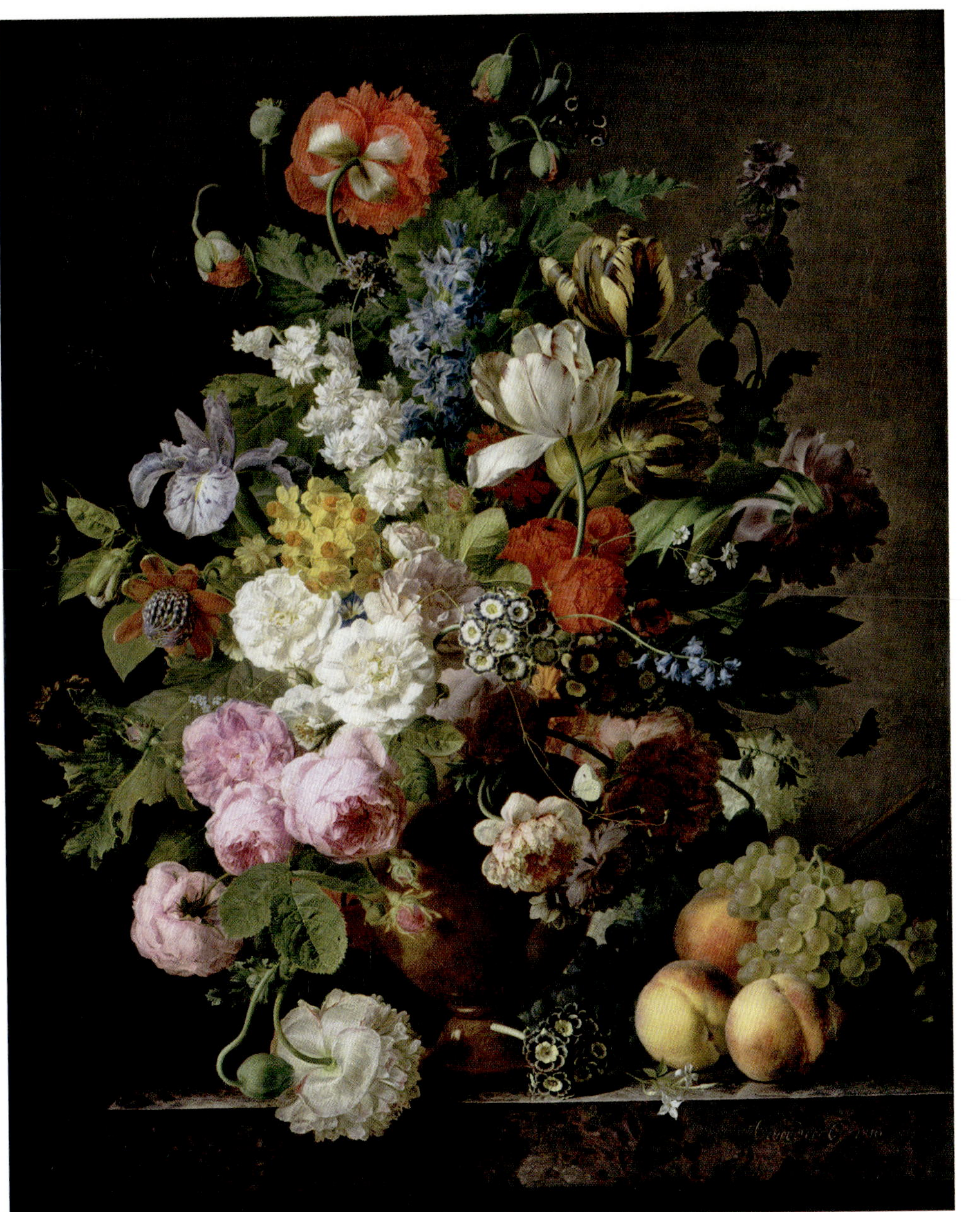

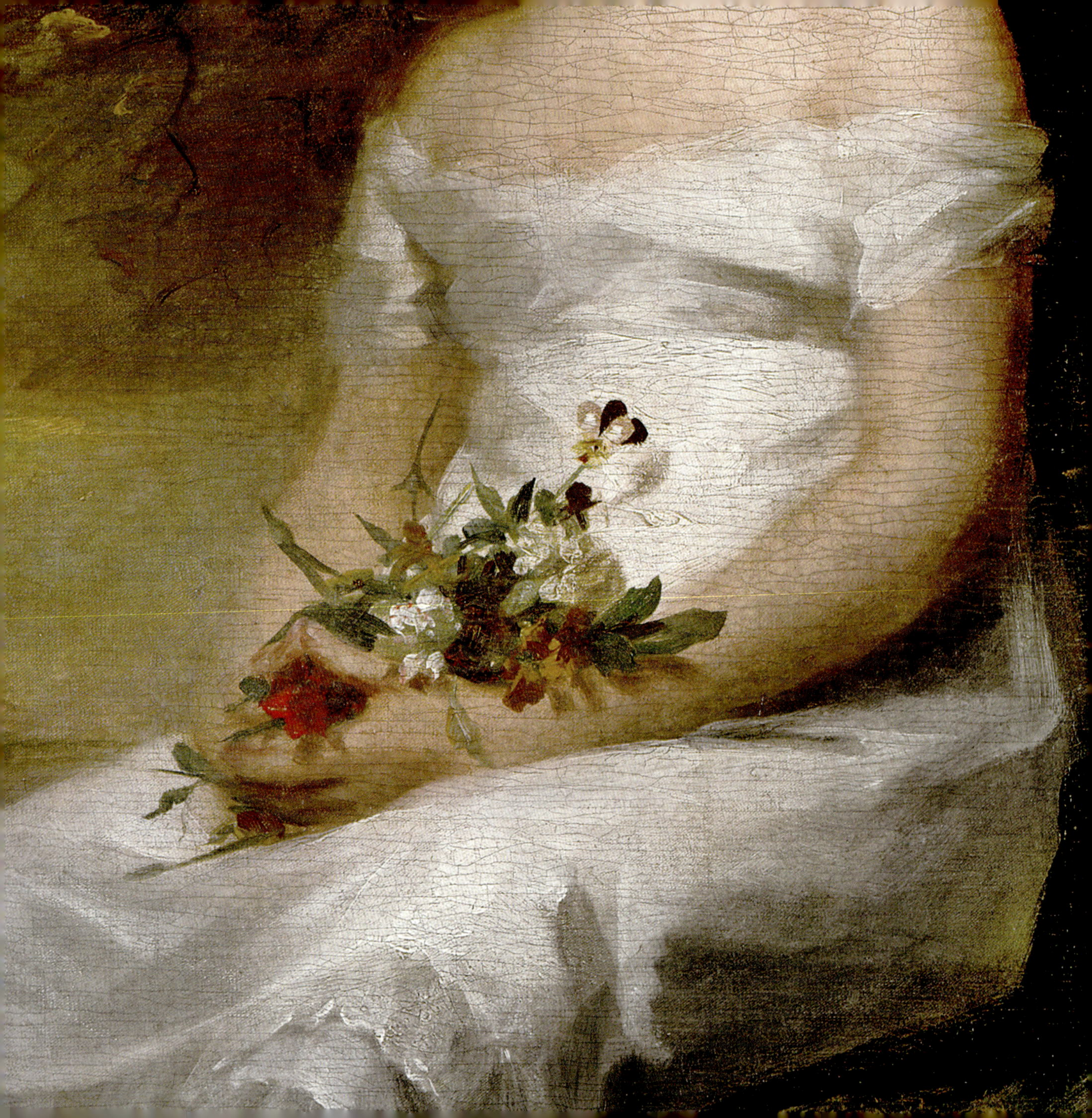

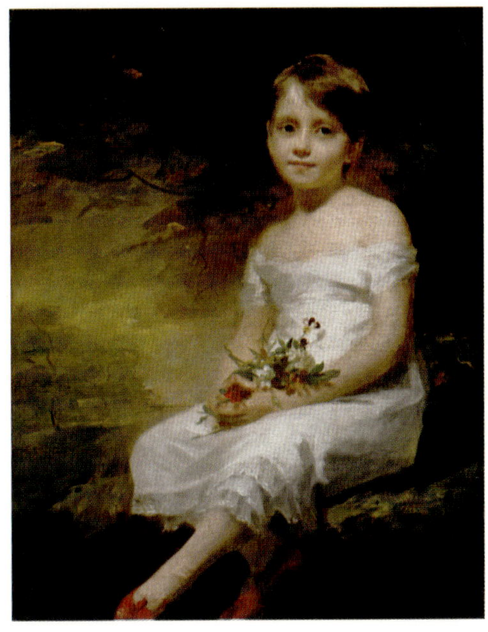

With an expression at once childlike, impish, and rather dreamy, Miss Nancy Graham adopts a graceful and unaffected pose. Wearing a white muslin dress with a becoming low neckline and her feet prettily shod in red, she seems to be getting ready to curtsy.

She nonchalantly holds a spray of mixed blooms that she seems to have just picked, perhaps from somewhere in the vast domain visible in the background. Skating over the details and emphasizing daring contrasts in light and shade, the artist's loose, nimble brushwork makes it no easy task to identify the species, but close examination at least reveals gillyflowers and pansies.

In the poetic language of flowers, the wallflower means liveliness, while the very name of the pansy of the field or garden (from the French *pensée*, "thought") evokes meditation. Perhaps this association can be interpreted as an allusion to the vivacity of childhood that the contemplative attitude of the young girl conceals? This portrait is sometimes entitled *Innocence* and then takes on broader allegorical significance. White is often linked with the purity of childhood and, echoed by the color of the dress, the pale gillyflowers, set off by a hint of purple in the petals, underline the candor associated with a person of tender years.

The life of Pierre-Joseph Redouté unfolded against a turbulent political backdrop: arriving in Paris in the reign of Louis XVI, he survived the Revolution, the Consulate, the Empire, and the Restoration, dying only during the July Monarchy. The scientific research that began in the Enlightenment was scarcely impeded by these political crises, and, while scientists were dispatched to the four corners of the world to collect plant specimens, in botanical gardens and natural history museums, chemists, botanists, and pharmacists were busy classifying and analyzing this new-found "material." Redouté made his own personal contribution to all this activity by portraying the world of plants with singular descriptive rigor. Preferring watercolor to gouache, his coloring acquired a new sense of life and mystery and his compositions gained considerably in freshness and vibrancy. He would first lay down the outline in black lead and then quickly wash in the watercolor, sometimes with a finishing touch in colored pencil. Modeling the forms in a delicate balance between light and shade, Redouté's palette was extremely delicate.

The accuracy of the drawing and the composition of this sophisticated bouquet comprised of anemone, pansies, daisies, and cyclamen, show that Redouté was not limited to documentary illustration.

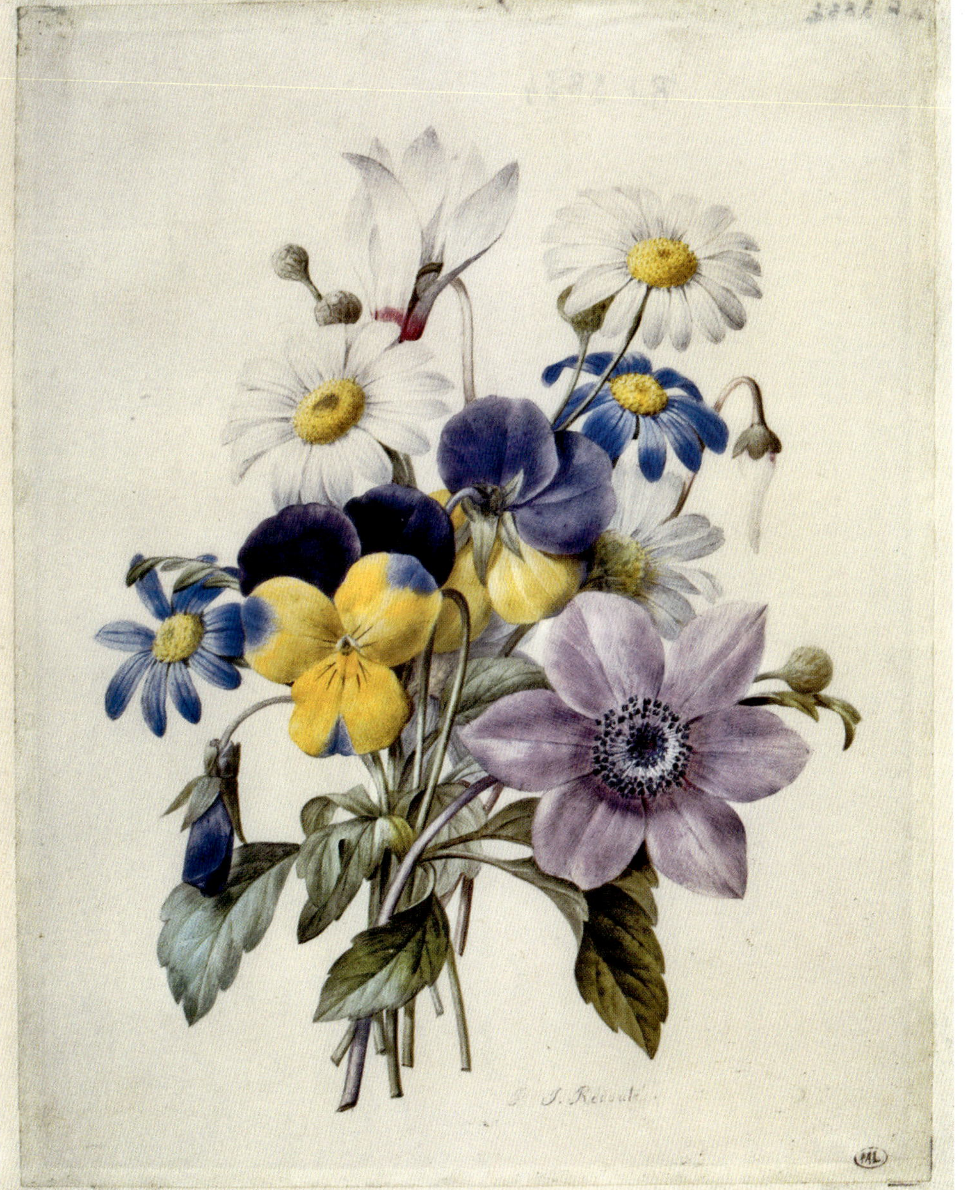

P. J. Redouté

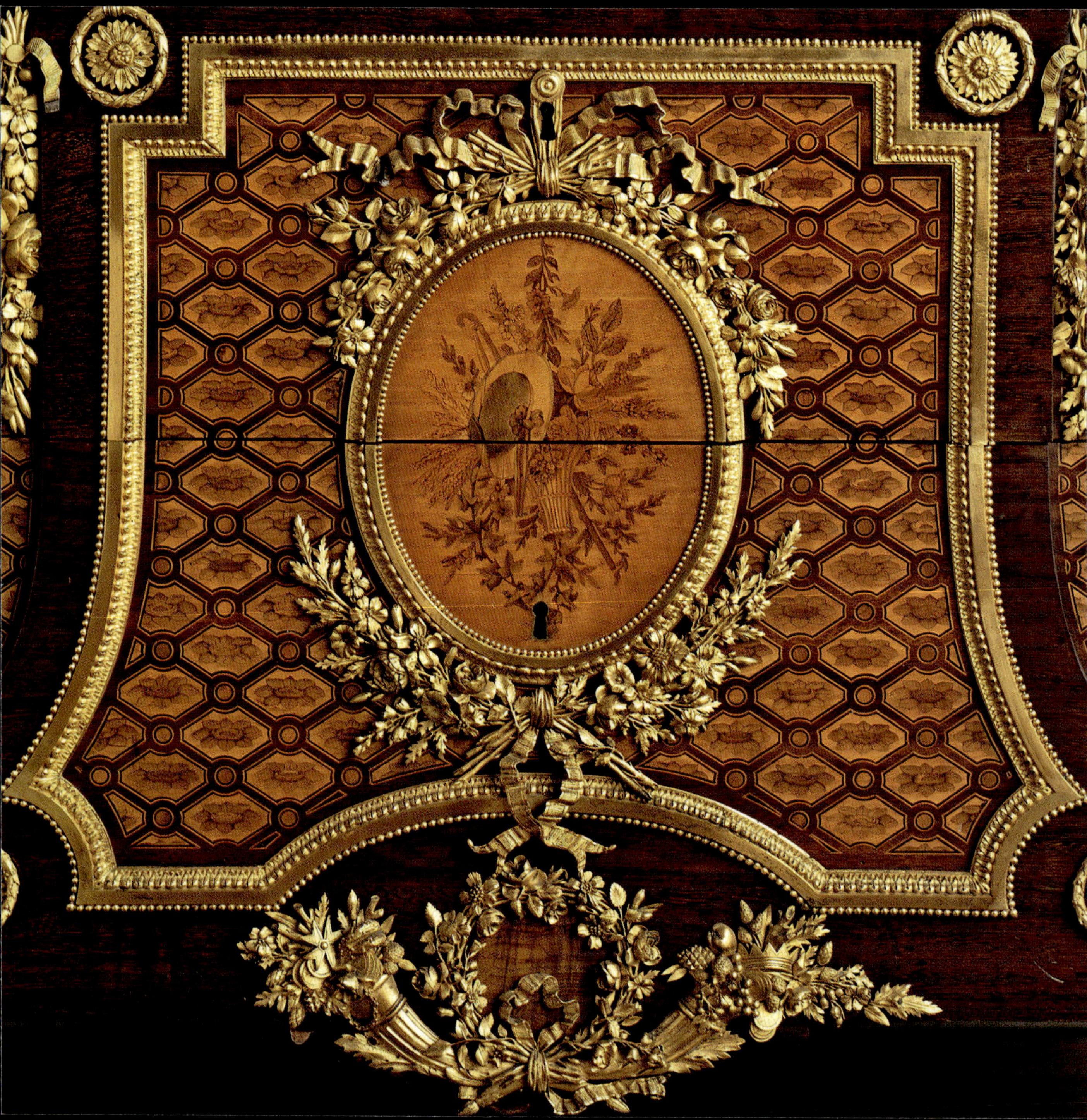

1. **JEAN-HENRI RIESENER** (1734–1806)
Commode, from the cabinet of Queen Marie-Antoinette, 1782
Marquetry of satinwood, purpleheart, sycamore, gilded bronze,
breccia of Aleppo marble, 34 ¼ x 45 x 20 in. (87 x 114 x 51 cm)

2. **ANDRÉ-CHARLES BOULLE** (1642–1732)
"Parrot" Armoire, n. d.
Inlay of ebony and purpleheart; inlaid with polychrome wood, brass,
tin, mother-of-pearl, horn; gilded bronze, 100 x 61 ¾ x 22 ¾ in.
(255 x 157 x 58 cm)

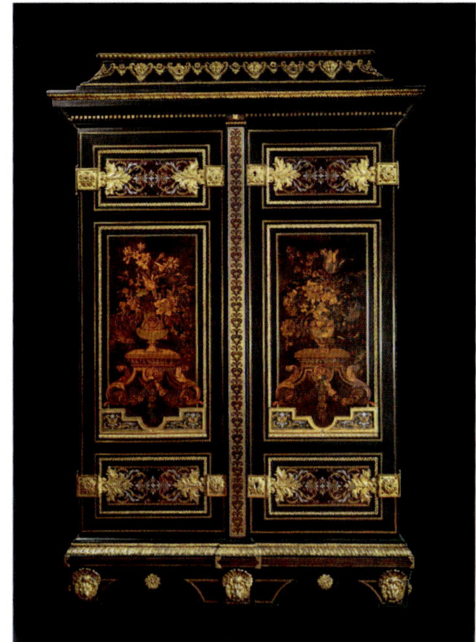

1. This *commode* chest was delivered
to Queen Marie-Antoinette on March 28,
1782, by Jean-Henri Riesener, furniture-
and cabinetmaker by appointment
to the French Crown, for the study next
to her chamber in the Château de Marly.
Especially admirable are the splendid
effects of light and shade in a marquetry
that forms a diamond-shaped lattice
pattern punctuated by circles.

The queen's fondness for nature
and for flower motifs is betrayed on
the medallion in the center, representing
a floral trophy with grasses; but even more
in the fabulous metalwork, whose

exceptional subtlety has more in common
with the chiseling of the silversmith than
with furniture bronzes. The flowers of the
field and the wheatears tied by ribbons
reflect the queen's penchant not only for
the countryside but also for high fashion.
She did really adore flowers, though:
the fabric from which her gowns were cut
and the textiles lining her apartments
were all decorated with them and she
would even stick a bloom or two into
her wig or straw hat when she played at
being a shepherdess in the park at Trianon.

PIERRE-PAUL PRUD'HON (1758–1823)
The King of Rome, 1811
Oil on canvas, 18 x 22 in. (46 x 56 cm)

In the midst of an unkempt yet protective landscape, like a demigod wearing the golden halo of the morning sun that peeps through the dense foliage, a naked child sleeps peacefully on the grass in a clearing. The three colors—the blue drapery on the right, the white linen on which the child reposes, and crimson coverlet—are those of France. Nature herself drives the point home and the plant symbolism indicates that this is no ordinary child: he is the heir to the Empire, son of Napoleon and Marie-Louise, who bore the title "King of Rome" from birth. Bottom right, we have myrtle, found all over the Mediterranean scrub and particularly in Corsica. This is one of the symbols of Venus and refers to the boy's mother, Marie-Louise, while the laurel in the background evokes Napoleon, the victorious general. On the left, at the foot of a tree-trunk, sprout fritillaries, also known in French as "imperial crowns." The two crimson-tinged blooms spreading over the sleeping infant recall the fact that he is a descendant of both the French and Austrian Empires. The painter, by bathing the scene in an at once harmonious and fantastical light that permeates both scenery and child, has transfigured what is an official portrait into pure poetry.

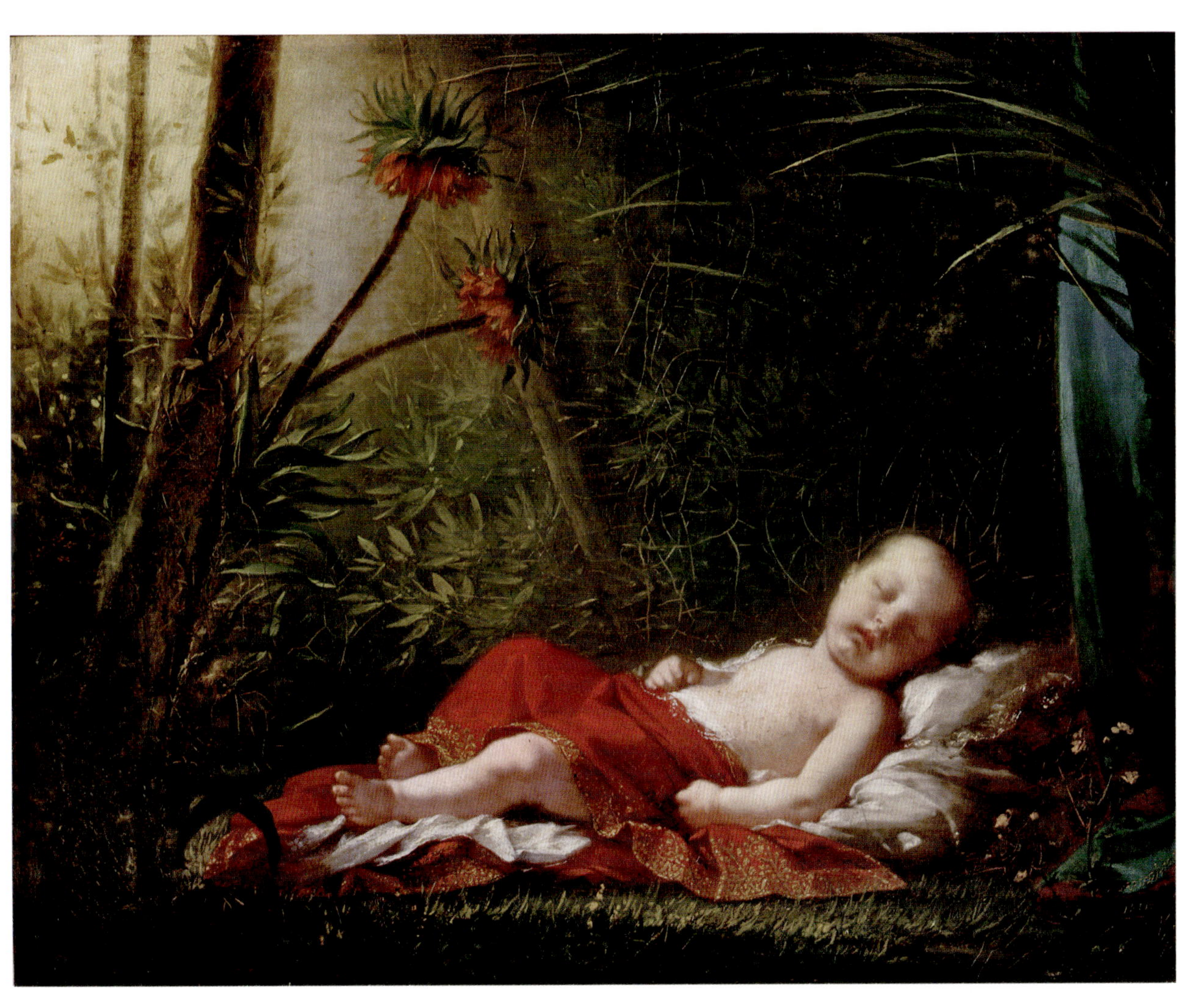

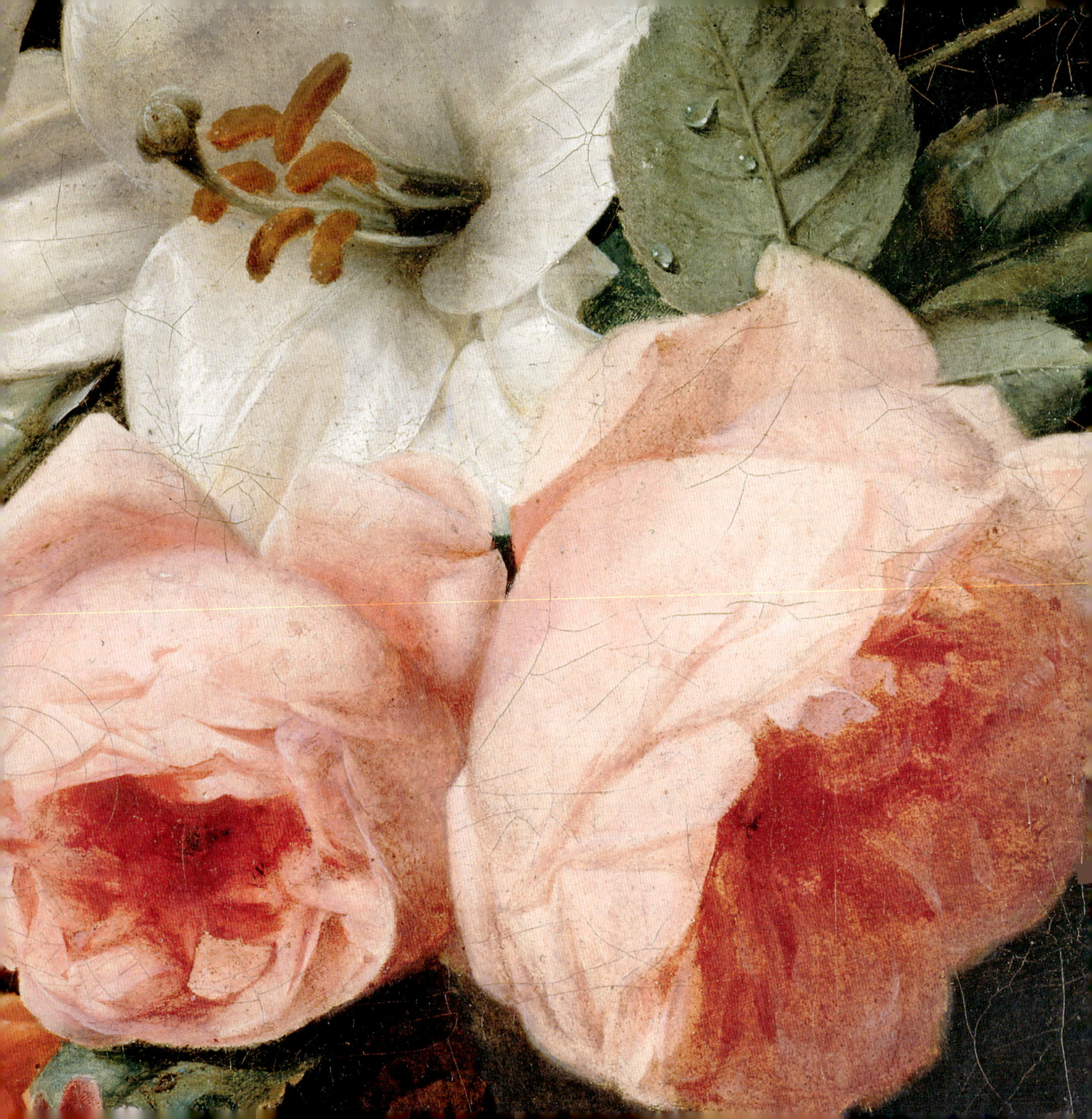

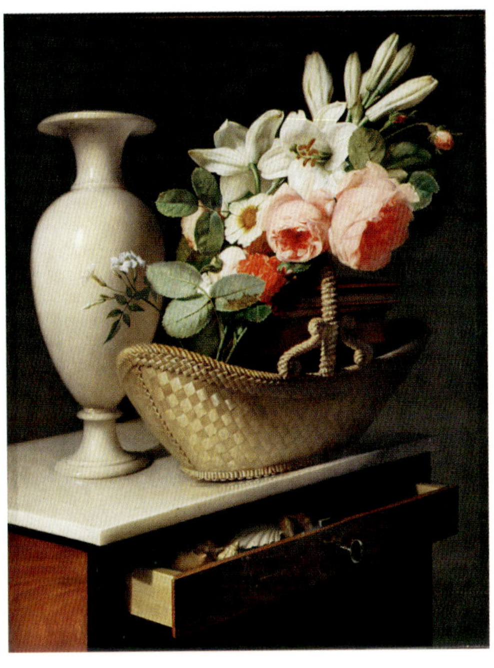

ANTOINE BERJON (1754–1843)
Bouquet of Lilies and Roses in a Basket Placed on a Chiffonnier, 1814
Oil on canvas, 26 x 19 ¼ in. (66 x 49 cm)

Antoine Berjon was an artist from Lyon, a flower painter of singular delicacy whose first trade—as a draughtsman of silk designs—shows through in smoothly handled paintings in light colors. Horticulture had by this time become more democratic, and the artist presents this simple bunch comprised of the heavy blooms of three cabbage (or Provence) roses, a lily stem, and a branch of orange blossom in an unpretentious straw basket. Arranged against a dark ground, the composition seems to surge out of the environing gloom. Whatever symbolic meaning still clung to the world of flowers had become decidedly more secular by the eighteenth century and the high moral tone of previous ages had almost evaporated. Interpretations now tended to focus primarily on the vicissitudes of love: thus, the rose, which up to that point had stood for the purity of the Virgin, now bears a full complement of thorns and stands for more human affections, half hopeful, half fearful.

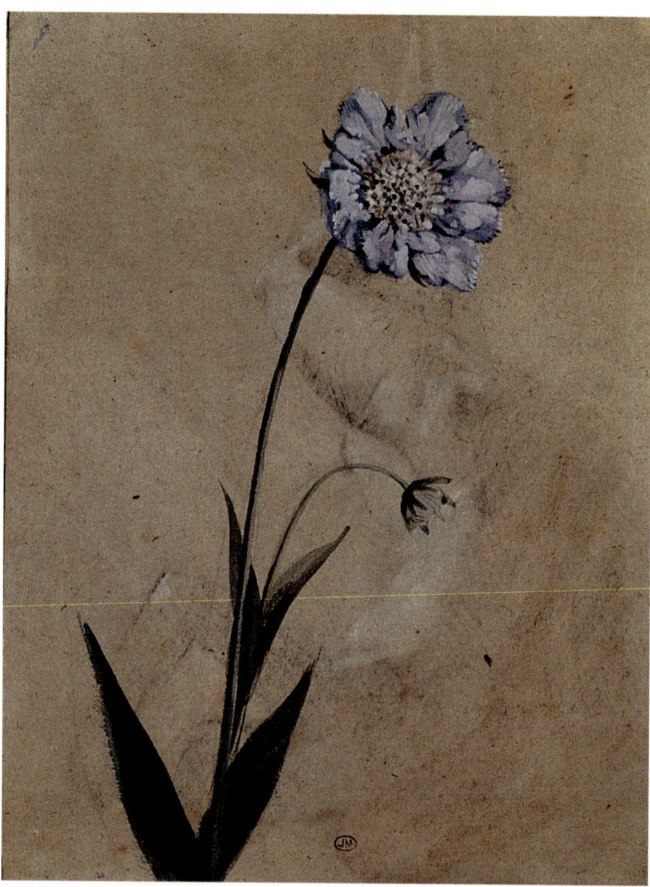

2. Among the Greeks the iris was a flower of mourning which was placed on a woman's tombs in tribute to the goddess of the same name. It was Iris who, having cut off a lock of hair from a woman's head as soon as she expired, would conduct her soul over to the land of the dead. Was it this ancient belief that inspired the young Delacroix to juxtapose a human skull drawn in black lead with two iris flowers painted in watercolor? We are rather of the opinion that the painter began by studying two flowers from nature, the macabre parallel being inspired by the general form of the specimen on the right: the drooping petal looks like a jawbone, while the exposed pistils are suggestive of a nasal cavity. Moreover, the closed part of the corolla on either side is redolent of the top of a skull.

Still, in the end the artist's conscious or unconscious motivations matter little: the combination of these two elements (skull and flowers) makes this sheet of studies into a veritable modern vanitas.

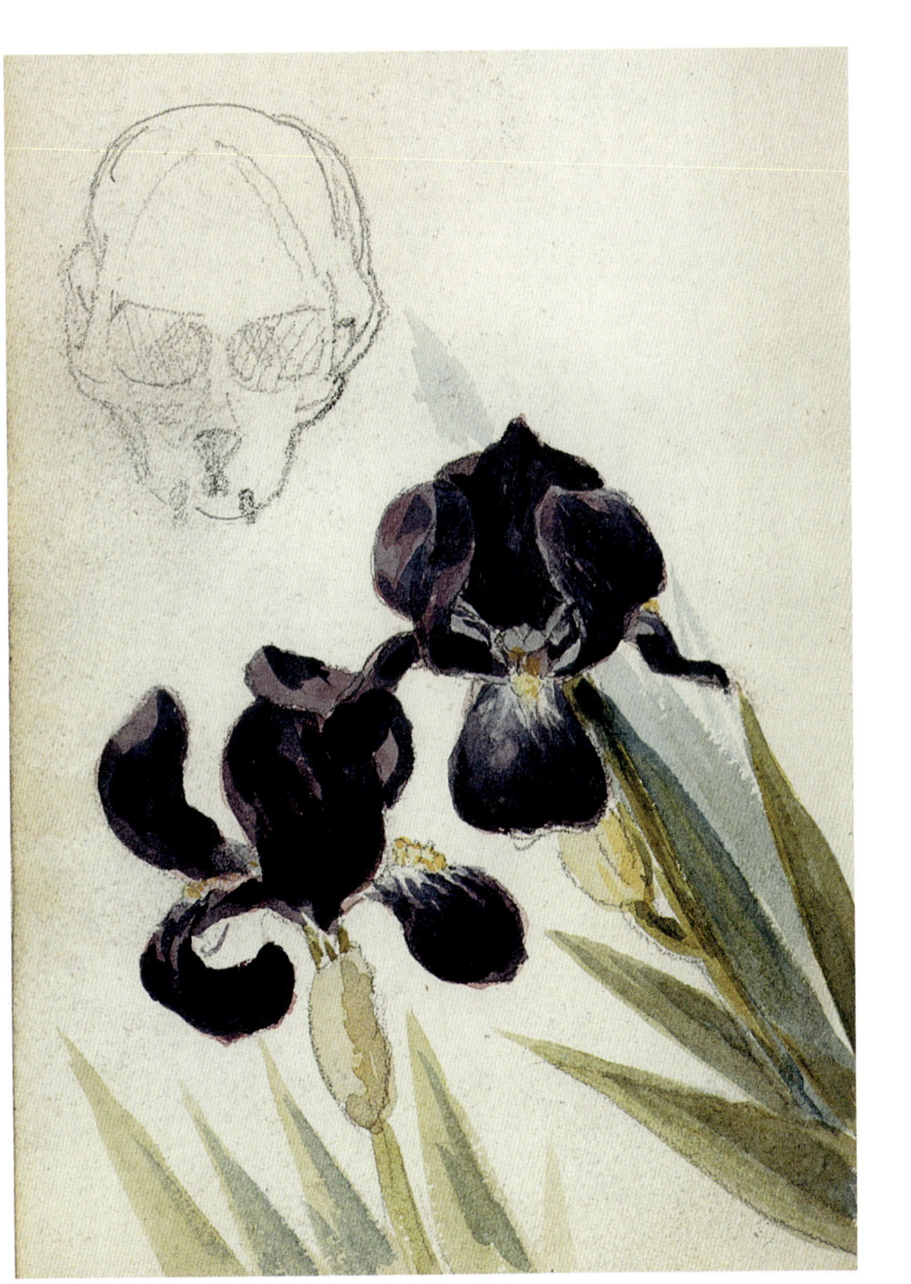

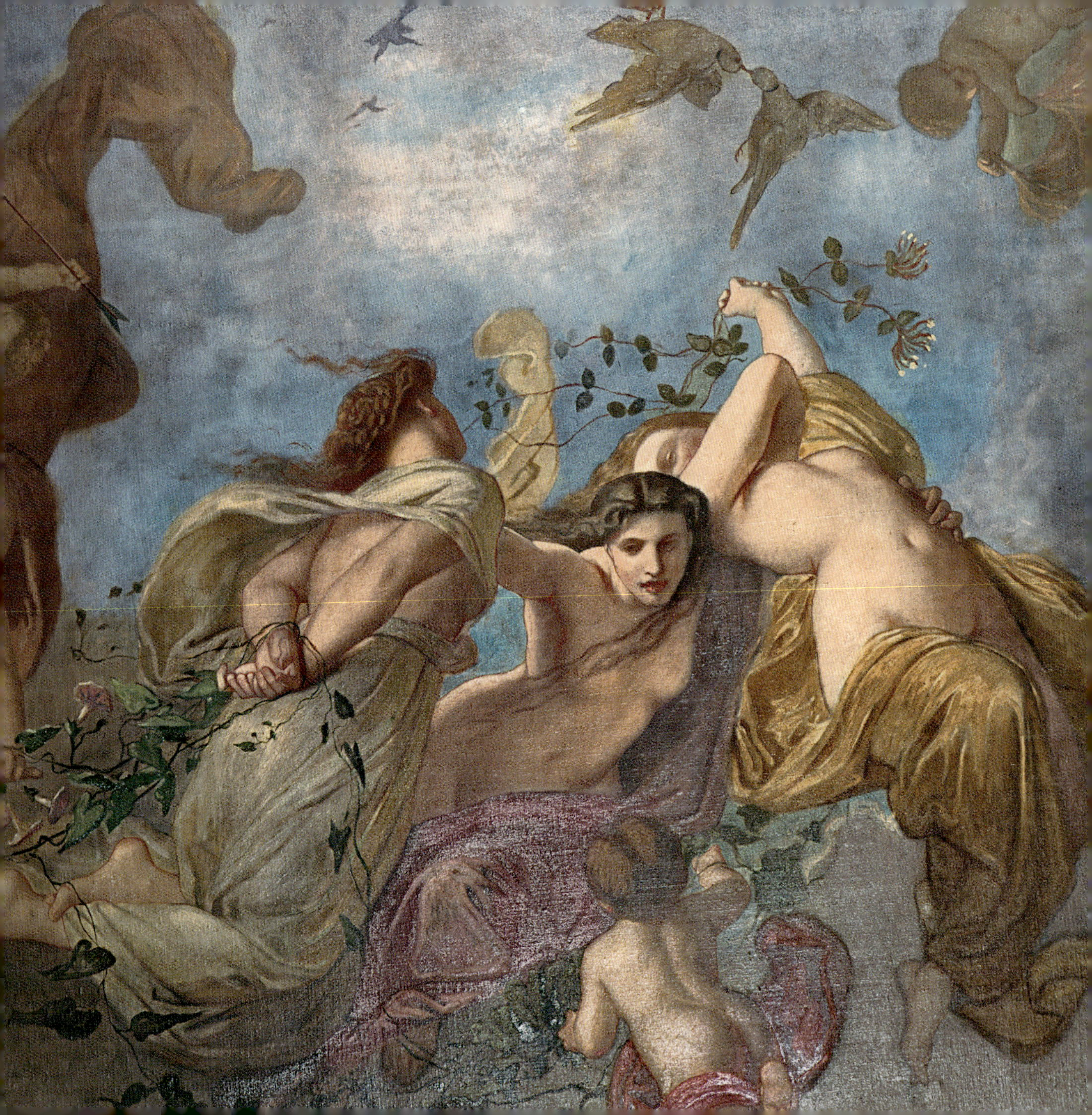

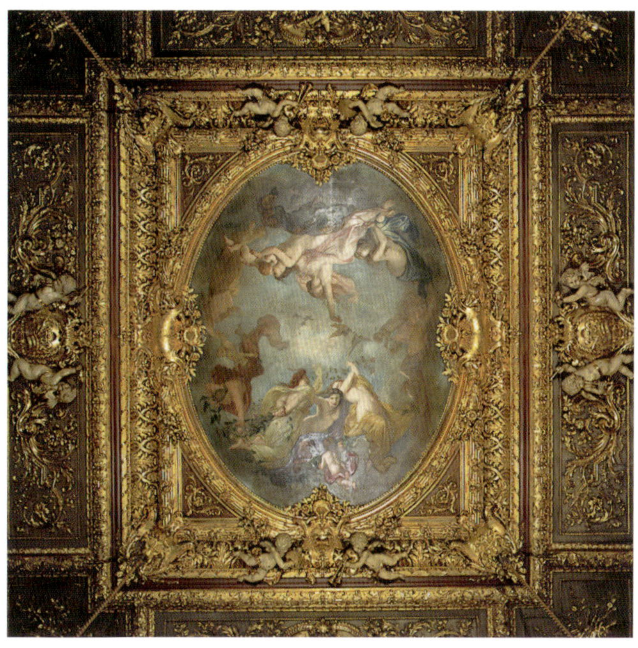

Between 1856 and 1861, the architect Lefuel was appointed to oversee the fittings for the interiors of the Ministry of State that had been assigned the new buildings that linked the Louvre to the Tuileries. It was on the ceiling in the drawing room-cum-theater whose entire décor is dedicated to flowers and music that Auguste Gendron painted this *Season of Flowers*. They scarcely leap out at one, though: flowers are not known to grow well in midair. Perhaps in the painter's mind the flowers he was thinking of were in fact the graceful nymphs, who seem to float weightlessly through the vaporous sky. What is more, if you look closely, three of these beauties entwine their arms as if to braid a garland to womanhood: one of them has her hands tied behind her back by a twist of convolvulus, while her blonde companion brandishes a trail or two of honeysuckle. Since they are species that cling and clamber around trees and trellises, bindweed and honeysuckle had become symbols of friendship and affection. Perhaps these adorable captives are the Seasons, shown flowing seamlessly one into the other.

Three roses in pastel tones seem to strike a pose in a narrow glass vase. They could almost be said to be just one and the same rose, shown from the front, rear, and in profile. Painted alone, with no surrounding decoration, they suffice in themselves and display their beauty against a neutral gray background, a simple arrangement that endows them with an astonishing sense of presence. Fantin-Latour deployed a fair amount of impasto on the petals and each corolla appears to stand up in relief against the briskly laid-in ground, under which one can make out the weave of the canvas. The verdigris hue and sketchy treatment of the leaves serves to link the flowers and the surface beneath. In the nineteenth century, many artists became literally obsessed with flowers: starting out as vehicles of symbolic meaning, then as subjects of observation, they were soon being painted solely for their intrinsic fragile beauty.

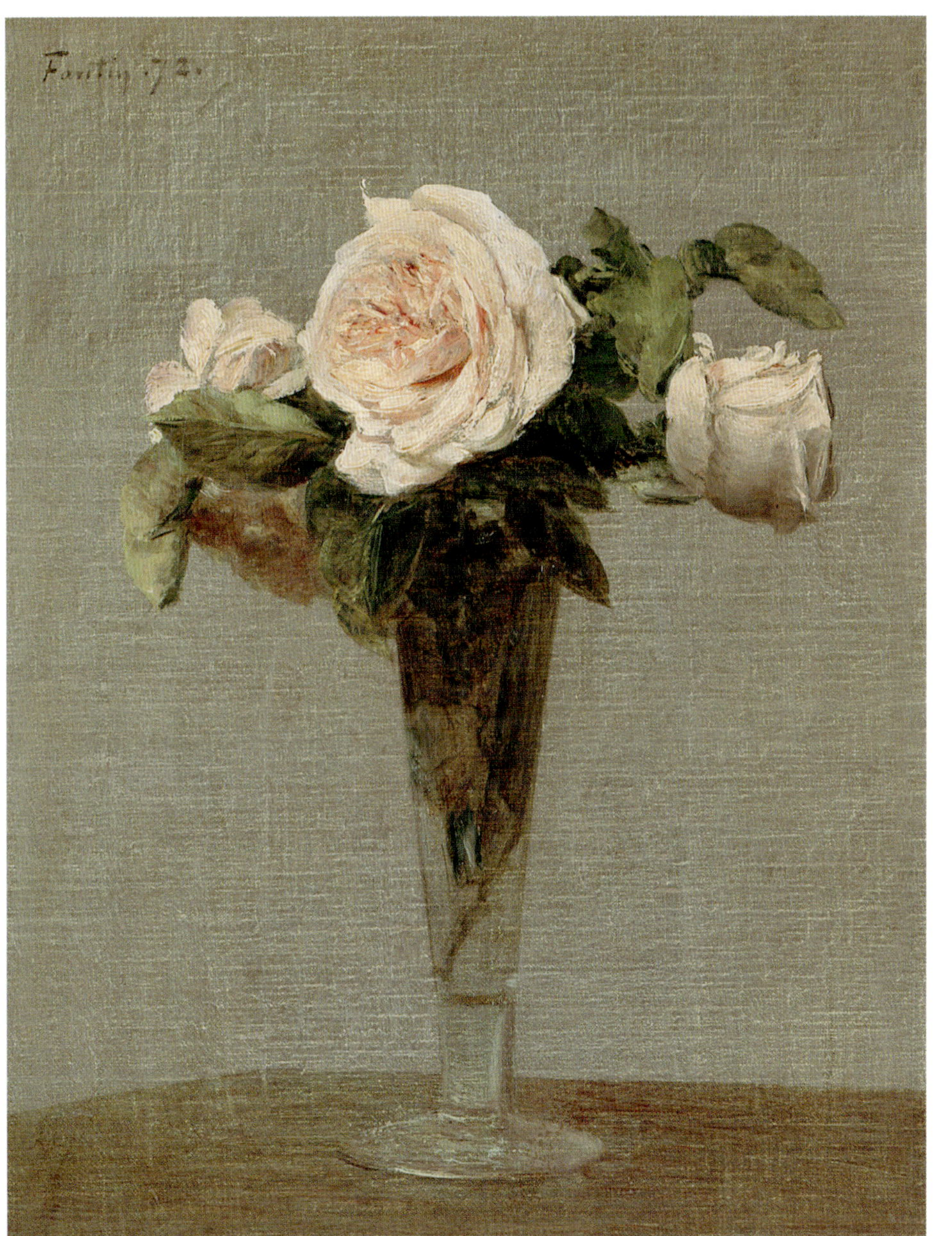

P. 10
*Wall painting, Woman smelling
a lotus flower*
1550–1295 BCE, Eighteenth Dynasty
Loess, straw, 13 ¾ x 10 ½ x 1 in.
(35 x 26.7 x 2.6 cm)
Inv. E 32565
Department of Egyptian Antiquities

P. 11
Stele of Lady Taperet
Tenth or ninth century BCE, Twelfth
Dynasty or Third Intermediate Period
Paint and varnish on wood,
12 ¼ x 11 ½ x 1 in. (31 x 29 x 2.6 cm)
Inv. E 52, N 3363
Department of Egyptian Antiquities

P. 12–13
*Relief from the Palace of Sargon II:
genius holding an opium poppy flower*
C. 710 BCE
Bas-relief, limestone, 4 ft. 8 ¾ in. x
3 ft. 10 in. (1.44 x 1.17 m)
Inv. AO 19869
Department of Eastern Antiquities

P. 14–15
*Preparing perfume from lilies; "Lirinon"
Relief from the tomb of Pairkep*
Reign of Psammetic II? (595–589 BCE),
Twenty-sixth Dynasty
Limestone, 11 ½ x 46 ¾ x 3 ¼ in.
(29 x 119 x 8 cm)
Inv. E 11377
Department of Egyptian Antiquities

P. 16–17
Fragment of a funerary stele, **known
as** *"The Exaltation of the Flower"*
C. 470–460 BCE
Parian marble, 22 ½ x 26 ¼ x 5 ½ in.
(56.5 x 67 x 14 cm)
Inv. MA 701
Department of Greek, Etruscan and
Roman Antiquities

P. 18
*Fragment of a floor mosaic: scattering
of roses and Phoenix*
Late fifth century CE
Marble and limestone, 19 ft. 8 ¼ in. x
13 ft. 11 ¼ in. (6 x 4.25 m)
Inv. MA 3442
Department of Greek, Etruscan
and Roman Antiquities

P. 20
Paving stone: Fleur-de-lis
Thirteenth–fourteenth century
Glazed earthenware, h. 5 in. (12.5 cm)
Inv. OA 12105-1, SN 626
Department of Decorative Arts

P. 21
Clasp decorated with a fleur-de-lis,
known as the *"Fermail de Saint Louis"*
Mid-fourteenth century
Silver-gilt, champlevé enamel,
semi-precious stones, h. 7 in.
(18 cm) approx.
Inv. MR 345
Department of Decorative Arts

P. 22–23
Antonio Puccio, *called* **Pisanello**
(c. 1395–1455)
Portrait of a Young Princess,
c. 1435–1440
Oil on wood, 17 x 11 ¾ in.
(43 cm x 30 cm)
Inv. RF 766
Department of Painting

P. 24
Diptych: Annunciation, St Christopher
Second half of the fifteenth century
Silver-gilt, ivory, 1 x 1 ¾ in.
(2.8 x 4.5 cm)
Inv. OA 52
Department of Decorative Arts

P. 25
Rogier van der Weyden
(c. 1399/1400–1464)
The Annunciation, c. 1440
Oil on wood, 33 ¾ x 36 ½ in.
(86 x 93 cm)
Inv. 1982
Department of Painting

P. 26
Albrecht Dürer (1471–1528)
A Flower, n. d.
Watercolor, pen, and brown ink,
11 ¾ x 5 ½ in. (30 x 13.7 cm)
Inv. 22 DR
Department of Graphic Arts

P. 27
Albrecht Dürer (1471–1528)
*Portrait of the Artist Holding a
Thistle,* 1493
Oil on wood, 22 x 17 ¼ in. (56 x 44 cm)
Inv. RF 2382
Department of Painting

P. 28
Raffaello Santi, *called* **Raphael**
(1483–1520)
*Madonna and Child with St. John the
Baptist,* **known as** *La Belle Jardinière,*
c. 1507–1508
Oil on wood, 48 x 31 ½ in. (122 x 80 cm)
Inv. 602
Department of Painting

P. 29
Bernardino Luini (1480/1490–1532)
Madonna and Child with an Angel,
known as the *Madonna of Menaggio,*
c. 1520–1530
Oil on wood, 31 ½ x 22 ¾ in.
(80 x 58 cm)
Inv. RF 2083
Department of Painting

P. 31
Mille fleur *tapestry: allegorical scene*
First third of the sixteenth century
Wool, silk, tapestry, 9 ft. 11 ¼ in. x 9 ft.
1 ¾ in. (3.03 x 2.79 m)
Inv. OA 11335
Department of Decorative Arts

P. 32
Anonymous
Pitcher with floral décor
Iznik (Turkey), c. 1560–1570
Quartz-frit ceramic, slip, glaze, paint
Inv. OA 7595
Department of Islamic Arts

P. 33
Anonymous
Dish with décor of swirling flowers
Iznik (Turkey), c. 1540–1555
Quartz-frit ceramic, décor painted
under the slip and the transparent glaze
Inv. OA 6740
Department of Islamic Arts

P. 35
Giuseppe Arcimboldo (1527–1593)
Spring, c. 1573
Oil on canvas, 30 x 25 in. (76 x 63.5 cm)
Inv. RF 1964-30
Department of Painting

P. 36–37
Tabletop
Seventeenth century
Hardstone inlay, 50 ¾ x 30 in.
(129 cm x 76 cm)
Inv. SN 768
Department of Decorative Arts

P. 38
Balthasar van der Ast (1593/1594–1657)
*Flowers, Shells, Butterflies, and
Grasshopper,* c. 1640–1650
Oil on wood, 20 ½ x 16 ½ in.
(52 x 42 cm)
Inv. RF 2001-1
Department of Painting

P. 39
Ambrosius Bosschaert (1573–1621)
*Bouquet of Flowers in a Stone Arch
Opening onto a Landscape,*
c. 1619–1621
Oil on copper, 9 x 6 ¾ in. (23 x 17 cm)
Inv. RF 1984-150
Department of Painting

P. 40–41
Domenico Zampieri, *known
as* **Domenichino** (1581–1641)
Daniel Seghers (1590–1661)
*The Triumph of Love in a Frame of
Flowers,* c. 1625–1627
Oil on canvas, 4 ft. 4 ¾ in. x 3 ft. 7 ¼ in.
(1.34 x 1.10 m)
Inv. 797
Department of Painting

P. 42–43
Nicolas Poussin (1594–1665)
Triumph of Flora, c. 1627–1628
Oil on canvas, 5 ft. 5 in. x 7 ft. 11 in.
(1.65 x 2.41 m)
Inv. 7298
Department of Painting

P. 44–45
Pieter Cornelisz van Slingelandt
(c. 1625/1630–1691)
Frans Meerman, Scrivener of the City
of Leyden with his Family, 1668
Oil on wood, 20 ¾ x 17 ¼ in.
(53 x 44 cm)
Inv. 1840
Department of Painting

P. 47
Abraham Mignon (1637–1679)
Flowers, Birds, Insects, and Reptiles, n.d.
Oil on wood, 19 x 16 ½ in. (48 x 42 cm)
Inv. 1554
Department of Painting

P. 48–49
Jean Belin, *called* **Blain de Fontenay**
(1653–1715)
Flowers in a Gold Vase, Bust of Louis
XIV, Horn of Plenty and Armor, 1687
Oil on canvas, 6 ft. 2 ¾ in. x
5 ft. 3 ¼ in. (1.9 x 1.62 m)
Inv. 4464
Department of Painting

P. 50–51
After a model by **François Girardon**
(1628–1715), **Jean-Balthazar Keller**
(**caster**) (1638–1702),
Philippe Magnier (1648–1715)
Aurora, c. 1686–1694
Bronze, 6 ft. 8 ¾ in. x 4 ft. 1 ¼ in.
x 3 ft. 7 ¾ in. (2.05 x 1.25 x 1.11 m)
Inv. MR 3243
Department of Sculpture

P. 52
Anonymous
Wild Rose,
Iran, eighteenth century
Gouache, 5 ¾ x 3 ¾ in. (14.6 x 9.4 cm)
Inv. MAO 158
Department of Islamic Arts

P. 53
Anonymous
Leaf from an album: The Arrival
of the Shah before the Great Mosque
of Dehli-Shajahanabad
India, Mughal School,
eighteenth century
Inv. MAO 2091
Department of Islamic Arts

P. 54
Anonymous
Box painted with a bunch of flowers,
Japan, n.d.
Inv. TH 377
Department of Decorative Arts

P. 55
Fragment of a curtain from the Grand
Salon at the Château d'Abondant,
c. 1750
Embroidery, painting on silk,
w. 5 ½ in. (13.7 cm)
Inv. OA 11790
Department of Decorative Arts

P. 56
Vincennes Manufacture
"Le Boitteux" Vase, 1755
Soft-paste porcelain, 11 x 9 ½ in.
(28 x 24 cm);
(including flowers: 12 ¼ x 13 in.
[31 x 33 cm])
Inv. OA 7608
Department of Decorative Arts

P. 57
François Boucher (1703–1770)
Girl Holding a Basket of Flowers, 1756
Pastel on parchment, 17 ¼ x 14 ½ in.
(44 x 37 cm)
Inv. 24813
Department of Graphic Arts

P. 58
Christiaen van Pol (1752–1813)
Vase adorned with bas-relief and
decorated with flowers
Miniature on enamel, 3 x 3 in.
(7.5 x 7.5 cm)
Inv. RF 197
Department of Graphic Arts

P. 59
Jan Frans Van Dael (1764–1840)
Vase of Flowers, Grapes and Peaches,
1810
Oil on canvas, 39 x 31 in. (99 x 79 cm)
Inv. 1196
Department of Painting

P. 60–61
Sir Henry Raeburn (1756–1823)
Little Girl Carrying Flowers,
also known as *Innocence,* n. d.
Oil on canvas, 35 ¾ x 28 in.
(91 x 71 cm)
Inv. RF 1962-15
Department of Painting

P. 63
Pierre Joseph Redouté (1759–1840)
Pansies and Marguerites, n.d.
Watercolor, 7 ½ x 5 ¾ in.
(19.3 x 14.8 cm)
Inv. RF 3834, recto
Department of Graphic Arts

P. 64
Jean-Henri Riesener (1734–1806)
Commode, from the cabinet of Queen
Marie-Antoinette, 1782
Marquetry of satinwood, purpleheart,
sycamore, gilded bronze, breccia
of Aleppo marble, 34 ¼ x 45 x 20 in.
(87 x 114 x 51 cm)
Inv. OA 12012
Department of Decorative Arts

P. 65
André-Charles Boulle (1642–1732)
"Parrot" Armoire, n. d.
Inlay of ebony and purpleheart; inlaid
with polychrome wood, brass, tin,
mother-of-pearl, horn; gilded bronze,
100 x 61 ¾ x 22 ¾ in. (255 x 157 x 58 cm)
Inv. OA 5516
Department of Decorative Arts

P. 67
Pierre-Paul Prud'hon (1758–1823)
The King of Rome, 1811
Oil on canvas, 18 x 22 in. (46 x 56 cm)
Inv. RF 1982-19
Department of Painting

P. 68–69
Antoine Berjon (1754–1843)
Bouquet of Lilies and Roses in a
Basket Placed on a Chiffonnier, 1814
Oil on canvas, 26 x 19 ¼ in.
(66 x 49 cm)
Inv. RF 1974-10
Department of Painting

P. 70
Eugène Delacroix (1798–1863)
Bound album: study of a scabious,
c. 1817–1826
Watercolor, brown paper, gouache
highlights, 6 ½ x 8 ½ in.
(16.7 x 22 cm)
Inv. RF 9141, folio 44 recto
Department of Graphic Arts

P. 71
Eugène Delacroix (1798–1863)
Bound album: Sketch of a skull
and two studies of irises, c. 1818–1823
Watercolor, lead pencil, 5 ½ x 3 ¾ in.
(13.7 x 9.5 cm)
RF 9153, folio 24 verso
Department of Graphic Arts

P. 72–73
Auguste Gendron (1817–1881)
The Season of the Flowers, 1860
Painted ceiling
Inv. RF 1993-30
Department of Painting

P. 75
Henri Fantin-Latour (1836–1904)
Flowers, 1872
Oil on canvas, 12 ¼ x 9 ½ in.
(31 x 24 cm)
Inv. RF 1961-39
Department of Painting

IN THE SAME SERIES